Satire
in the Comedies of
Congreve, Sheridan, Wilde, and
Coward

Satire
in the Comedies of
Congreve, Sheridan, Wilde, and
Coward

By

ROSE SNIDER

PHAETON PRESS

NEW YORK

1972

Originally Published 1937
Reprinted 1972

Published by PHAETON PRESS, INC.
Library of Congress Catalog Card Number - 79-159119
ISBN - 87753-055-6

FOREWORD

The English comedy of manners might plausibly be regarded as a type of literature that does not faithfully reflect the life of its time. The reason is twofold: in the first place, it is decidedly limited in characterization and setting, dealing as it usually does with the smart set of London, and, in the second place, it is apt to be very artificial. But scope has nothing to do with validity, and artificiality is not always inconsistent with realism. As for the latter point, Charles Lamb was surely wrong in saying, in his famous essay *On the Artificial Comedy of the Last Century,* that the comedy of manners of the Restoration is "altogether a speculative scene of things, which has no reference whatever to the world that is." It was artificial, of course, but so was the society that it professed to exhibit. At any rate, it had one characteristic element that made it significantly representative, namely, satire. And in this respect every successful comedy of manners may be considered representative. It is true that one may enjoy satire without approving of the thrust; but, on the whole, the satire offered in popular plays may be deemed good evidence of the tastes of the audience, of the attitude of the audience toward life. In this view lies the justification of the present study of the satire in the English comedy of manners during different periods.

The selection of the periods was easy, since the English comedy of manners has had its day only three times—in the Restoration period, in the decade in the second half of the eighteenth century when Goldsmith and Sheridan flourished, and in the modern period beginning with Oscar Wilde and continuing with Noel Coward to date. The choice of distinguished and representative dramatists in these periods was equally easy, since Congreve in the first period was unquestionably preëminent, Sheridan in the second period was almost alone, Wilde brilliantly revived the type toward the close of the nineteenth century, and Coward is among the cleverest and most popular of those still carrying on. Of the four, Congreve and Coward are the most representative, for Sheridan did not so much reflect the taste of his time as lead a revolt against it, and Wilde represented nothing so much as he represented Wilde; yet the dra-

iii

matic successes of even the latter two have much significance as social phenomena.

Miss Snider has done her work with great thoroughness, and has shown a marked aptitude for the recognition and analysis of satire. I believe that nothing of importance in the field that she has explored has escaped her notice. The final result is not only an interesting study of the drama but also a social document of no little significance.

Stanley R. Ashby

TABLE OF CONTENTS

ACKNOWLEDGMENT

I am indebted to Dr. Stanley R. Ashby, of the University of Maine, for the careful supervision of this study; and to Dr. Milton Ellis, of the University of Maine, for the encouragement and the many helpful suggestions he has given me since I began my graduate work.

INTRODUCTION

It is the purpose of this study to call attention to satire in the comedies of William Congreve, Richard B. Sheridan, Oscar Wilde, and Noel Coward. To include all four dramatists, the discussion takes, as its limits, the dates 1693—the presentation year of Congreve's first play, *The Old Bachelor*—and 1936—the year of Coward's latest contribution to the theatre, nine short plays grouped as *Tonight at 8:30*. The actual years under consideration, however, restrict the scope to the distinctly dramatic periods of the writers, namely, 1693-1700, 1775-1779, 1892-1895, and 1920-1937. The type of drama chosen for this study is the comedy of manners, which more than any other type is concerned with satire. It is the function of such drama to present a criticism of society, and satire is one of the most effective methods of criticism available to the dramatist.

The four dramatists have been selected because they represent the periods of the greatest success of the comedy of manners. The aim in covering so much ground is to enable the reader to view the progress of satire within the precincts of the comedy of manners, where it is most evident. Having thus gained the perspective, the reader will notice more readily the differences in the comedies, differences which vary with the times and according to the conditions under which the comedy of manners flourished. When these variations have been observed, the satirical element in the comedy of manners should stand out conspicuously and link the drama of Congreve with that of Coward.

Of the various species of the comic spirit, satire is one of the most important, yet it is very often overlooked. Most dissertations on comedy give little more than passing attention to satire. Occasionally it receives comment under the general topic of humor and is thereupon dismissed. This study intends to give particular consideration to satire as a quality in itself apart from wit and humor, with which it is so closely allied. By the expert use of satire, one most nearly approaches the spirit of high comedy, for then, and only then, does comedy appeal to the intellect and awaken Meredithian laughter.

The Merriam-Webster *Dictionary* of 1934 defines satire as "a literary composition holding up human or individual vices or follies, or abuses or shortcomings of any kind, to reprobation by means of ridicule, derision, burlesque, or other method of intensifying incongruities, usually with an intent to provoke amusement." The laughter brought about by satire, however, is not always that of genuine amusement. Where satire enters into pure comedy, the robust laugh frequently occasioned by the latter is replaced by a cynical smile. Meredith puts it thus: "If you detect the ridicule, and your kindliness is chilled by it, you are slipping into the grasp of Satire."[1] The fact that the reactions to satire are intellectual rather than emotional provides Allardyce Nicoll with a basis for distinguishing between the moralist and the satirist, for "the true moralist appeals nearly always to the feelings and not to the intellect, and the satirist rarely plays upon the emotions."[2] There are times when the satirist, in ridiculing the weaknesses of society, unintentionally comes close to being a moralist, for, in deriding these existing follies, he may indirectly be advancing reforms. Satire is an adult ridicule, superseding the childish taunt; at its best, it is an admission and reflection of the frailties of society.

Satire is one of the least tangible of literary devices. Often it is felt but not seen, experienced but not visualized. This is particularly true of the play on the stage, wherein the action moves forward so rapidly that the underlying thought frequently escapes the audience, or, when it is evident, soon ceases to appear significant. In reading a play, however, one has more time for perusal of striking passages and for reflection upon the playwright's ideas. There is in the comedy of manners a frankness which embraces satire as its greatest ally. The particular brand of satire involved is not the biting, often uncouth, variety of Swift, nor the purely ironical type of Defoe. It is a satire in which the criticism is crisp and sprightly, and alleviated by genuine humor. It is characteristically polite and gives evidence of good breeding. This politeness may or may not be affected, but it is there, nevertheless. George Jean Nathan maintains that "Polite comedy...is polite only as a servant is polite, that is, for business reasons."[3] Be that as it may,

---

[1] Meredith, George, *An Essay on Comedy*, p. 133.

[2] Nicoll, Allardyce, *An Introduction to Dramatic Theory*, p. 149.

[3] Nathan, George Jean, *Art of the Night*, p. 22.

it is the variety of satire found in this polite comedy which helps to make the name, comedy of manners, an appropriate as well as an attractive one.

Congreve, coming early in this survey, was the first to perfect the comedy of manners. After Congreve's achievement, this comedy went into a decline from which it was not roused until late in the eighteenth century, when it fell into the hands of the young Sheridan. To save it from dwindling into the sentimental banality which was rife on the eighteenth-century stage, Sheridan endowed it with some of the Restoration spirit, occasioning a brief renaissance for the Congrevean type of drama. Sheridan, then, marks the second climax in the history of the comedy of manners; and, though incapable of producing work superior to that of his master, he did, nevertheless, write plays approximately equal to Congreve's as literary successes. The greater part of the nineteenth century, dominated by Victorian morality and earnestness, was not in a mood to respond to the sophisticated satires of Congreve and Sheridan. Gradually, however, the old spirit began to permeate society, until in the mauve decade Oscar Wilde came into a somewhat dubious prominence. His talent for satirical and witty writing merited him a place of honor at a respectful distance from his two predecessors. The twentieth century, still comparatively young, has already indicated a marked preference for the comedy of manners, which has found its best expression in Noel Coward. Coward seems to have recaptured Congreve's sense of sophistication and satire, Sheridan's plot-creating ability, and Wilde's knack for clever phrases. To these he has added a twentieth-century rapidity of style and his own flair for smart talk and novel effects.

The plays to be considered in this discussion are comedies of manners. They reproduce the life of a particular coterie, high in the social scale, with much leisure time on its hands, a condition conducive to the cultivation of the intellect. Thus, the members of this set are engaged in a perpetual contest of wit, and may the best man win. As is often the case, the "best men" in this game of wits are few, and the situation is found to be in the hands of the would-be wits, who devote their time to memorizing similes and epigrams with which to astonish their tolerant friends. Women hold an important place in such a world of wit, for this type of comedy is possible only in a progressive society where both sexes are on equal terms. There is an added zest to the repartee when men match their wits against those of the opposite sex and find the challenge an exciting and not always an easy one.

The comedy of manners seems to have flourished best in the hands of youthful playwrights who have known when to stop writing. Congreve's comedies were written from 1693 to 1700, and after the latter date, which marks the presentation of *The Way of the World,* he retired from the theatre at the age of thirty. At twenty-eight, four years after his first success, Sheridan gave up the drama for a political career. Wilde's dramatic period was of even shorter duration, extending from 1892 to 1895, when he was a little over forty. Coward started writing plays in 1920, when he was twenty-one, and at present his activity shows no signs of abating, for which fact modern drama should be duly grateful.

Their youthfulness should not be held against these playwrights, for, although young in years, they were well versed in the ways of the world. They found their audiences civilized enough to appreciate criticism, and, accordingly, they utilized their most important weapon—Satire.

CHAPTER I

WILLIAM CONGREVE

The comedy of manners, in order to succeed best, must be in the hands of a playwright who is himself one of the social set which he portrays. It is a realistic type of drama, and in order to achieve for the audience an orthodox view of this particular clique, he must be of it to know whereof he speaks and to reproduce accurately its speech and manners. Belonging to a distinguished family, Congreve[1] was well fitted to write of the company in which he moved, but the ambition to be a man of fashion conflicted for a time with the desire to be a great writer. Ewald has observed:

> Either object was within his reach. But could he secure both? Was there not something vulgar in letters—something inconsistent with the easy, apathetic graces of a man of the mode?...In his youth the desire of literary fame had the mastery; but soon the meaner ambition overpowered the higher, and obtained supreme dominion over his mind.[2]

He was, however, more fortunate than some playwrights. Thus, when he saw that the trend of the times was away from the typical Restoration drama, he could remark cynically regarding his dramatic achievement that "but little of it was prepared for that general taste which seems now to be predominant in the palates of our audience."[3] He then retired from the drama to lead the easier life of a gentleman and wit. After the trying combat with Jeremy Collier, which represented a definite change in the attitude of the theatre public, Congreve was content to call it a day. On this basis, he is not to be censured for his famous, though perhaps apocryphal, remark to Voltaire, that he wished "to be visited on no other footing than as a gentleman who led a life of plainness and simplicity."[4]

---

[1] The plays of Congreve on which the discussion in this chapter is based are *The Old Bachelor* (1693), *The Double-Dealer* (1693), *Love for Love* (1695), and *The Way of the World* (1700). The dates are those of presentation.

[2] Ewald, A. C., *William Congreve*, p. xii.

[3] Dedication to *The Way of the World*.

[4] Quoted by Ewald, *op. cit.*, p. xxxvi.

Congreve, young as he was when he wrote his comedies, was wise beyond his years in his insight into human character. He himself was a member of the artificial society which he depicted, but his dislike of hypocrisy and affectation was never so strong that he felt constrained to pick up the cudgels of reform. Seeing through the superficiality of the people around him, he was content merely to point it out. At heart he was not a reformer. Even his reply to Jeremy Collier, in which he attempted to prove that each play carried with it a constructive moral, was weak and half-hearted, for the morals expressed in the closing lines were never so convincing as the contents of the plays themselves.

Congreve was not seriously concerned about society's "going to the dogs." He was, no doubt, aware of it, but he dismissed the idea as another instance of the way of the world. There are always Jeremy Colliers to worry about such affairs. Congreve was unfortunate only in that the purging of the stage had to come just at the time when he was achieving his greatest success. He was not a fighting man. Accordingly, after arguing in a gentlemanly fashion, he withdrew from the fray to devote himself to the witty company which he loved, and to the gout which he could not ignore.

William Congreve is an example of Restoration gentleman *par excellence.* Of his own encounters with women, little is known other than that Anne Bracegirdle and the Duchess of Marlborough filled important places in his life. The former represented his love for the theatre; the other, his admiration for the nobility. In commenting upon the poet's bequest of ten thousand pounds to the Duchess, who did not need it, rather than to Mrs. Bracegirdle, who did, Zoltán Haraszti expresses the opinion that "Congreve, the last Cavalier in English literature, thus asserted the aristocracy of writing, before authorship became a profession."[5]

In replying to adverse criticism of *The Double-Dealer,* Congreve explained his general attitude toward the ladies, although it may be suspected that his tongue was in his cheek all the while.

> But there is one thing at which I am more concerned than all the false criticisms that are made upon me, and that is, some of the ladies are offended. I am heartily sorry for it, for I declare I would rather disoblige all the critics in the world, than one of the fair sex.

---

[5] Haraszti, Zoltán, *More Books,* Vol. IX, No. 3, March, 1934, p. 95.

They are concerned that I have represented some women vicious and
affected: how can I help it? It is the business of a comic poet to
paint the vices and follies of humankind; and there are but two sexes,
male and female, men and women, which have a title to humanity;
and if I leave one half of them out, the work will be imperfect. I
should be very glad of an opportunity to make my compliment to
those ladies who are offended;...[6]

With Congreve, women achieve a new importance. He credits them with having as high a mentality as the men, and with being
equally capable of guiding their own lives. In his comedies he goes
further than this, and proves that man can be really powerless in
the hands of the superior woman he was fond of portraying. This
is evident in *The Way of the World,* wherein Millamant has Mirabell twisted about her little finger. He is content if she will but
confess she loves him. In *Love for Love* Valentine and Angelica
are in a similar situation; Angelica has the upper hand and actually
drives Valentine to feign madness in order to prove his love for
her. Bellmour and Belinda present a somewhat weaker version of
the same thing in *The Old Bachelor,* and in *The Double-Dealer* even
Cynthia is represented as a more dominating character than Mellefont, her lover.

Without a doubt, Anne Bracegirdle served as the model for
these four heroines, for in their characters is to be found Congreve's
greatest expression of poetry and beauty. In creating the leading
men and fixing their status in regard to their ladies, perhaps Congreve had in mind himself and his own relationship to Anne. Over
these loves there hovers a certain sense of futility, which reminds
one of Congreve's own affair. When he finally forsook the theatre, he gave up Anne too, for she was the crystallization of all his
dramatic ideals of womanhood. Although his own love affair did
not end happily, Congreve at least managed to provide satisfactory
outcomes for his characters. His "Utopia of gallantry,"[7] as Lamb
called it, must be perfect in every way.

There is, of course, an element of satire to be found in the
tactics of Congreve's women. In regard to the heroines the satire
is hardly that of serious ridicule; on the contrary, one feels it is

---

[6] Epistle Dedicatory to *The Double-Dealer.*

[7] Lamb, Charles, *The Essays of Elia,* "On the Artificial Comedy of the
Last Century," p. 278.

merely that of mild amusement. He does not expose them with the intention of chastizing them, but for the sake of providing a laugh at their expense.

It is characteristic of Congreve that he never introduces his heroines before the second act, and generally not before the second scene of that act, reserving the preceding scenes for the men. When the women appear, the exposition has been completed, and all is ready for unimpeded action. Another example of Congreve's technique in the conservation of time is his handling of the love situation itself. We are never permitted to watch the falling-in-love process itself, for that which we do witness is a finished product. It is taken for granted that the love is there. However, one becomes so much interested in speculating upon the methods of pursuit and in anticipating the obvious solutions that one does not regret having been excluded from the preliminary clashes.

There is no doubt about Belinda's love for Bellmour, or Araminta's for Vainlove. The audience has been acquainted with this fact as early as the perusal of the cast of characters. Both women have practically the same views on love, but Belinda is not so willing to admit what Araminta talks about casually. Araminta plays the game as well as she can and is satisfied with the results. Belinda considers such action beneath her, but at heart she too delights in the excitement of the chase if she can but have the upper hand. How lightly she dismisses Araminta's accusations of her love for Bellmour!

> *Aram.* . . . You don't know that you dreamed of Bellmour last night, and called him aloud in your sleep.
> *Belin.* Pish! I can't help dreaming of the devil sometimes; would you from thence infer I love him?
> *Aram.* But that's not all; you caught me in your arms when you named him, and pressed me to your bosom.—Sure, if I had not pinched you till you awaked, you had stifled me with kisses.
> *Belin.* O barbarous aspersion![8]

In commenting upon this haughty lady and her attitude toward her lover, Dobrée maintains: "There is already something of Congreve's final excellence in Bellmour and Belinda, precursors of Mir-

---

[8] *The Old Bachelor*, II, 2.

abell and Millamant."[9] Indeed, Belinda, in her desire to make Bellmour conform to her wishes, is but Millamant on a smaller scale.
We can almost hear her echoing the words of her superior in the
scene wherein she instructs Bellmour in the art of love:

> *Belin.* Prithee, hold thy tongue!—Lard, he has so pestered me
> with flames and stuff, I think I shan't endure the sight of a fire this
> twelvemonth!
> *Bell.* Yet all can't melt that cruel frozen heart.
> *Belin.* O gad, I hate your hideous fancy! you said that once be-
> fore.—If you must talk impertinently, for Heaven's sake let it be with
> variety; don't come always, like the devil, wrapped in flames.—I'll
> not hear a sentence more, that begins with an "I burn"—or an "I
> beseech you, madam."
> *Bell.* But tell me how you would be adored; I am very tract-
> able.
> *Belin.* Then know, I would be adored in silence.[10]

And Bellmour, always ready to oblige, immediately resorts to sign
language, or, as Belinda terms it, "dumb rhetoric."

Araminta, on the other hand, is far more frank and even goes
so far as to admit that "If love be the fever which you mean, kind
heaven avert the cure! Let me have oil to feed that flame, and
never let it be extinct, till I myself am ashes!"[11] Thus we are provided with sufficient contrast, although Araminta is presented only
as the usual "confidante" and background for the lady who must
be won. Araminta taunts her own lover until at last he is forced
to beg forgiveness of her, and she is satisfied, for Vainlove is once
again in her power. Belinda, on the contrary, is the typical Congrevean lady of beauty and refinement who, by means of her virtue
and aloofness, keeps her lover enthralled.

Heroine number two is Cynthia, loved by and in love with
Mellefont, but, since this play is dominated to a great extent by the
double-dealing Maskwell, Cynthia has little occasion to indulge
in feminine caprices in order to test Mellefont's love. The power
of Cynthia over Mellefont is such that he is willing to marry her

---

[9] Dobrée, Bonamy, *Restoration Comedy, 1660-1720*, p. 126.
[10] *The Old Bachelor*, II, 2. Here, as in other of the passages quoted from
Congreve and Sheridan, the reader will notice the lavish use of commas and
the occasional disregard for capitalization which are characteristics of seventeenth and eighteenth century writing.
[11] II, 2.

Finally we come to Millamant, that paradox of affectations and virtues which enchanted Congreve. To be sure, she too is in love, but she must be wooed; and since she is so far above all other women, the wooing must likewise be of a superior sort. The ordinary stratagems whereby women are compelled to yield are not for her. Her evaluation of herself is neither over- nor underestimated. She knows she possesses an innate power for attracting men, and attracting them is a favorite pastime with her. Since most men bow to beauty, what can be expected of them when they are confronted by a superior mentality as well? Millamant is one of those coquettes whose every whim has been indulged by fascinated, even envious, admirers of both sexes. She is a lady at all times, and, in thinking of her, one never forgets this. There are few Millamants in the world, but even the minority manage to hold the lesser mortals in complete subordination. The women who boast of being their friends are far below them in every respect. Occasionally a man appears with whom such persons can be on an equal plane, and Mirabell approaches the requirements most nearly.

In Congreve's successive plays preceding *The Way of the World,* one can almost see the playwright sketching in the outlines of the heroines. First there is Belinda, but she is too vague. With Cynthia, fuller strokes achieve a more definite outline. Angelica presents a still more satisfying picture, and approximates reality. Millamant, however, is an exception to the rule, for she fairly breathes of life and emotion. She is so vivid that we are almost tempted to stretch out a hand to touch her and be thrilled; and when we find she is not there, we must with regret surrender her to Lamb's world.

Mirabell tried to analyze her character, but he finally concluded that the unusual combination of faults and virtues resulted in a strange perfection, and, Endymion-like, he was content to humble himself before her splendor. As he explains to Fainall:

> *Mir.* . . . for I like her with all her faults; nay, like her for her faults. Her follies are so natural, or so artful, that they become her; and those affectations which in another woman would be odious serve but to make her more agreeable. I'll tell thee, Fainall, she once used me with that insolence, that in revenge I took her to pieces; sifted her, and separated her failings; I studied 'em, and got 'em by rote. The catalogue was so large, that I was not without hopes one day or

other to hate her heartily: to which end I so used myself to think of
'em, that at length, contrary to my design and expectation, they gave
me every hour less and less disturbance; till in a few days it became
habitual to me to remember 'em without being displeased. They are
now grown as familiar to me as my own frailties; and in all prob-
ability, in a little time longer, I shall like 'em as well.[16]

This from Mirabell, the man of the world! That a man of Mirabell's sophistication should permit a woman thus to circumscribe
his life was something which called for more than mere dallying
about for the duration of a play; indeed, it required sterner stuff
of a loftier mien which would in turn provoke the Meredithian response in "thoughtful laughter." Thus, Congreve's turn of mind
finds satirical possibilities in the sorry spectacle presented by the
anxious sophisticate playing vainly at counterpoint with the assured
and self-confident lady who makes the world's way what it is. The
irony of it appealed to Congreve again and again, until in this play
he exhausted the subject and gave it up to concentrate on other
topics.

Millamant is not really heartless; she but prefers to appear so
since it was the fashion of the day. Congreve, like many another,
had realized that woman's place was not merely in the home; that,
in fact, the two sexes were on equal terms. It is this characteristic
which marks Congreve's age as having achieved greater heights in
the scale of civilization, and Millamant represents the new woman
asserting her recently acquired rights. That cruelty of which she
is accused by Mirabell is only a part of the perfected technique of
the coquette, for at heart she knows that after a time she will give
in to him. It is only to put him in his proper place and to make him
realize her importance. Thus we have them arguing pleasantly:

> *Mrs. Mil.* ... Now I think on't I'm angry—no, now I think on't
> I'm pleased—for I believe I gave you some pain.
> *Mir.* Does that please you?
> *Mrs. Mil.* Infinitely; I love to give pain.
> *Mir.* You would affect a cruelty which is not in your nature;
> your true vanity is in the power of pleasing.
> *Mrs. Mil.* Oh I ask your pardon for that—one's cruelty is one's
> power; and when one parts with one's cruelty, one parts with one's

---

[16] *The Way of the World*, I, 2,

power; and when one has parted with that, I fancy one's old and ugly.[17]

Mirabell suspects what she is really doing, but, nevertheless, he is forced to admit that Millamant is playing the winning hand in this love game. Again:

> *Mrs. Mil.* ...Well, I won't have you, Mirabell—I'm resolved— I think—you may go.—Ha! Ha! Ha! what would you give, that you could help loving me?
> *Mir.* I would give something that you did not know I could not help it.[18]

In truth, the man is on the rack, wincing each time she laughs at his sincerity. To complete the scene, there is Mirabell's oft-cited confession of his weakness:

> *Mir.* ....Think of you? to think of a whirlwind, though 't were in a whirlwind, were a case of more steady contemplation; a very tranquillity of mind and mansion. A fellow that lives in a windmill, has not a more whimsical dwelling than the heart of a man that is lodged in a woman....To know this, and yet continue to be in love, is to be made wise from the dictates of reason, and yet persevere to play the fool by the force of instinct....[19]

Toying with irresolution is Millamant's greatest crime where Mirabell is concerned.

It is evident from this review of the leading women of the comedies that Congreve was dangling before the eyes of his public the comical spectacle of the man in love, subjected to the tortures inflicted upon him by his loved one, yet unable to put an end to them even by pleading vainly with her. It is satire, but the type of laughter occasioned by it has a note of sadness in it.

When we consider the other women who delight in moulding the lives of men, we find no longer the poignant touch which was so apparent in the portrayal of Belinda, Cynthia, Angelica, and Millamant. In regard to these lady villains, one feels that Congreve has settled down to the more serious business of true satire,

---

[17] II, 2.
[18] II, 2.
[19] II, 2.

for, at the close, he too seems to be relieved at washing his hands of the persons he has ridiculed.

First of all there is Silvia, in *The Old Bachelor*. She has been jilted by Vainlove, and for revenge must ensnare the gullible fool, Heartwell. Even her maid Lucy inherits some of her spitefulness, as the following couplet reveals:

> Man was by nature woman's cully made;
> We never are but by ourselves betrayed.[20]

Such a remark is sufficient to prepare us for the ensuing interference of this "other woman," and we are not too much surprised at the ease with which she deceives the old bachelor into thinking her innocent and capable of returning his love. Her pretense lures him on until he yields and promises to return with a parson. Silvia's reaction to this is at once evident as she exclaims: "Ha! ha! ha! an old fox trapped!"[21] Were it not for the fact that Bellmour is a good friend of Heartwell's, the latter would truly have been caught. As it is, Bellmour merely is having a little fun at his friend's expense. Nor are we sorry when Silvia, in turn, is trapped into marriage with the wittol Sir Joseph, who admits somewhat ruefully that, "thanks to my knighthood, she's a lady."[22]

It is in *The Double-Dealer* that Congreve lets us see to what extremes a woman can go when her passions have been trifled with. It may seem unfair to consider this play in the same light as the others, for it is a sort of changeling among the comedies of Congreve, having in it both comic and tragic elements. Yet, since the subject under consideration is the power of women over men, a discussion of the play is pertinent. Here, then, it is Lady Touchwood, Mellefont's aunt, who upsets the relatively smooth course of events in the lives of her nephew and Cynthia. Mellefont is aware of her violent passion for him, but can do nothing to avert it.

Lady Touchwood is not a typical Congrevean character. On the contrary, she is much better fitted to associate with the temperamental duchesses of the sensational dramas of James Shirley or John Ford. Possessing a venomous nature, she can think of nothing

---

[20] *The Old Bachelor,* III, 1.
[21] III, 4.
[22] V, 5.

but revenge, and this craving for vengeance is what makes her akin to those women of the late Elizabethan tragedies. She has the characteristics of a female Machiavellian protagonist and can sow the seeds of suspicion like an Iago. But Lady Touchwood reckons each time without the double-dealing Maskwell. His interference makes her attempts at ruining Mellefont doubly hard, for Maskwell's affection for her has long since worn off.

First, with great subtlety, she imparts to her husband the fact that Mellefont is being more than a nephew to her. This is sufficient to arouse Lord Touchwood, although there is little he can do to alter the situation other than working himself up to a frenzy. Mellefont is the one who suffers most, for he is being ill-treated by Maskwell as well as by his aunt. The cruellest part of the affair with Lady Touchwood is the scene wherein Mellefont is led to believe he has her at his mercy, when in reality she is only dissembling in order to gain time. When at the crucial moment Maskwell brings in Lord Touchwood, the latter deems his wife's tears to be signs of pleading for her honor, which is as she had intended. Her alibi for Mellefont is that he has gone mad, and her husband is loyal enough to ignore his nephew and listen to his wife.

Just when Maskwell is about to succeed in his plan to wed Cynthia, Lady Touchwood learns how she herself has been deceived by him. Her line of action has been disrupted:

> *Lady Touch.* ...Shame and distraction! I cannot bear it. Oh! what woman can bear to be a property? To be kindled to a flame, only to light him to another's arms! Oh, that I were fire, indeed, that I might burn the vile traitor! What shall I do? how shall I think? I cannot think.—All my designs are lost, my love unsated, my revenge unfinished, and fresh cause of fury from unthought-of plagues.[23]

Congreve, however, is not the playwright to allow a play to end unhappily. Lady Touchwood and Maskwell are revealed in their true light, but not until after Lady Touchwood has threatened to kill her false lover. Lord Touchwood is given an opportunity to display his manliness by rewarding the "virtue and wronged innocence" of Mellefont and Cynthia.

---

[23] *The Double-Dealer,* V, 2.

One other woman is allowed full rein of power in this play, and that is Lady Plyant. In regard to this lady there is genuine satire, for she is that type of woman who always presents opportunity for humor. When Lady Touchwood falsely represents to Lady Plyant that Mellefont loves her, Lady Plyant, unusually credulous by nature, is at once convinced and tells her husband, Sir Paul, about it. He is all for challenging Mellefont at once, but is subdued by his wife.

> *Lady Ply.* 'Tis my honour that is concerned; and the violation was intended to me. Your honour! You have none but what is in my keeping, and I can dispose of it when I please;—therefore don't provoke me.
> *Sir Paul (Aside).* Hum, gadsbud, she says true!—(*Aloud*) Well, my lady, march on, I will fight under you, then; I am convinced, as far as passion will permit.[24]

Both are certain that Mellefont is making Cynthia the means of procuring Lady Plyant, and yet it is evident that the lady is flattered by the mere idea. The scene in which she interrupts by denials and refusals Mellefont's attempts to explain, presents an extremely amusing situation for the audience. For example:

> *Mel.* Madam, pray give me leave to ask you one question.
> *Lady Ply.* O lord, ask me the question! I'll swear I'll refuse it! I swear I'll deny it!—therefore don't ask me: nay, you shan't ask me; I swear I'll deny it. O gemini, you have brought all the blood into my face!...
> *Mel.* Nay, madam, hear me; I mean—
> *Lady Ply.* Hear you! no, no; I'll deny you first, and hear you afterward. For one does not know how one's mind may change upon hearing....[25]

This misunderstanding continues for some time until Mellefont realizes it must be the doing of his aunt.

Another instance of her ascendancy appears shortly thereafter when a boy arrives with a letter for Sir Paul. All his letters must first be perused by her. Sir Paul excuses this to Careless as "a humour of my wife's; you know women have little fancies."[26] Her

---

[24] II, 1.
[25] II, 1.
[26] III, 2.

power over Sir Paul is so great that when, through a mistake, he
intercepts a note from Careless to her, she persuades him that she
was but testing his love for her, and such is his dog-like faith in
her that he believes her, while she continues her flirtation with Careless.   This is the sort of thing Congreve never overlooks in his
search for a laugh.   The doting husband who is blind to his wife's
indiscretions is ever food for satire, whereas the folly of the wife's
indiscretions comes in for its share as well.

There are scheming women in *Love for Love* also, but they
never dominate the men entirely.   In *The Way of the World* we
have something of the same situation that we found in *The Double-
Dealer,* only this time it is not the hero's aunt who has a passion for
him, but the aunt of the heroine.   Since this passion has not been
returned by him, she feels justified in seeking revenge.   As in the
other play, the aunt's power lies in her ability to prevent her niece's
marriage to the man they both love.   But Lady Wishfort is not the
dragon Lady Touchwood is.   Her barbs lie not so much in what
she does as in what she says.   Her "flow of boudoir billingsgate,"[27]
as Meredith terms it, is the most dangerous thing about her, and,
consequently, her verbal attacks are not greatly feared.   Like Lady
Touchwood, she too meets with defeat, but she is far more gracious
than the former.

We have thus cursorily surveyed the outstanding women of
Congreve's plays, and have attempted to convey some impression
of his ideas regarding them.   Apparently, Congreve was of the opinion that the weaker sex was thriving on the new nourishment of
equality with the opposite sex and thus gaining strength.   At any
rate, the fact remains that in the plays of Congreve woman's position has been elevated to heights hitherto seldom attained, and by
this means she approaches most nearly the sophisticated, modern
woman of today.   In this way, points in common between the playwright of 1700 and that of 1937, or, more specifically, between
William Congreve and his newest disciple, Noel Coward, are established.

When we turn our attention to Congreve's satirical treatment
of the follies of women, we think first of Lady Froth, who, as he
explains in the "Dramatis Personae," is "a great Coquette; pre-

---

[27] *Op. cit.,* p. 101.

tender to poetry, wit, and learning." Whenever she appears, the audience is ready for an amusing scene. No doubt, Lady Froth was one of the contributing factors which led to the belief, on the part of the female audience, that *The Double-Dealer* was a deliberate satire on their sex. But Congreve assured them that he was merely trying to present a complete picture of that particular society which would be imperfect were the ladies neglected.

Lady Froth is never weary of telling the world about her love for Lord Froth, and her frequent discussion of her love at once leads one to question her sincerity in this regard. Her pretensions to learning make her all the more ridiculous, and the idea occurs that perhaps in Lady Froth is to be found that seed which comes to greater fruition in Lady Wishfort, and finally blossoms forth in Sheridan's perfected Mrs. Malaprop. The scene in which she is commenting on the merits of her husband is an admirable one:

> *Lady Froth.* ...I think I may say he wants nothing but a blue ribbon and a star to make him shine, the very phosphorus of our hemisphere. Do you understand those two hard words? if you don't, I'll explain 'em to you.
> *Cyn.* Yes, yes, madam, I'm not so ignorant.—(*Aside.*) At least I won't own it, to be troubled with your instructions.
> *Lady Froth.* Nay, I beg your pardon; but being derived from the Greek, I thought you might have escaped the etymology.—But I'm the more amazed to find you a woman of letters, and not write! bless me! how can Mellefont believe you love him?[28]

And the heroic poem which she is composing in honor of Lord Froth is outrageously entitled "The Syllabub," with Lord Froth in the leading role as "Spumoso." This makes her flirtation with Brisk all the more amusing, until at the last even Lord Froth becomes slightly suspicious of his ultra-amorous spouse. The passage wherein Brisk and Lady Froth confess their passions for each other is brimful of laughter which can not but prove contagious when heard from the stage.

It appears that this aptitude for double-dealing applies not only to Maskwell, but to Lady Froth and Lady Plyant as well.

The successful satirist never indicates specifically that any particular foible of society is ridiculous, or that it should be corrected.

---

[28] *The Double-Dealer,* II, 1.

On the contrary, his aim is merely to copy society with its faults and its virtues; and, by holding it up in a mirror, as it were, he thus creates the same effect in a far more subtle manner. He credits the audience with being capable of recognizing their weaknesses. He is likewise not seriously interested in whether or not society attempts to alter the existing situation. His only desire is that they understand and laugh with him. Subconsciously, perhaps, he hopes that his writing may have some influence in making the world a better place to live in, but seldom will the satirist admit even to himself anything of the kind. He is a denizen of another sphere, and he looks down cynically upon the inhabitants of the lower plane.

Thus Congreve, in creating Lady Wishfort, is but holding up for inspection Exhibit A in the case of satirist versus woman. She is the butt of Congreve's satire on old age trying to talk itself into being young again. According to Mirabell, Lady Wishfort is fifty-five years old. Unwilling to grow old gracefully, she insists on flattering herself that the marks of age upon her are very slight. How incensed she becomes at Foible's report that Mirabell has referred to her as "superannuated frippery!" And yet she is forced to face the truth when she looks into her glass. Foible consoles her:

> *Foib.* Your ladyship has frowned a little too rashly, indeed, madam. There are some cracks discernible in the white varnish.
> *Lady Wish.* Let me see the glass—Cracks, sayest thou?—Why, I am errantly flayed—I look like an old peeled wall. Thou must repair me, Foible, before Sir Rowland comes, or I shall never keep up to my picture.[29]

There is a poignant touch, a note of sadness, in this portrait of decaying womanhood. That sudden girlish coyness which she affects in her anticipation of romance with Sir Rowland is indeed a contradictory side to her personality when viewed in comparison with her more usual boldness. Her youth is so far away that she has long since forgotten how to act when being wooed, and is now making her debut all over again. How excitedly she rehearses the manner in which she shall greet Sir Rowland:

> *Lady Wish.* Well, and how shall I receive him? in what figure shall I give his heart the first impression? there is a great deal in the

---

[29] *The Way of the World,* III, 1.

first impression. Shall I sit?—no, I won't sit—I'll walk—ay, I'll
walk from the door upon his entrance; and then turn full upon him—
no, that will be too sudden. I'll lie—ay, I'll lie down—I'll receive
him in my little dressing-room, there's a couch—yes, yes, I'll give
the first impression on a couch.—...Hark! there's a coach.[30]

And then when Sir Rowland finally arrives, though he is the servant
Waitwell in disguise, she summons to her aid all her Malapropish
diction. No "boudoir billingsgate" is evident here, for now she is
concerned with the creation of a favorable impression of her—dare
we say—charms? She is inordinately humble and dependent upon
him, ready to agree to anything he says.

> *Lady Wish.* Well, Sir Rowland, you have the way—you are no
> novice in the labyrinth of love—you have the clue.—But as I am a
> person, Sir Rowland, you must not attribute my yielding to any sin-
> ister appetite, or indigestion of widowhood; nor impute my com-
> placency to any lethargy of continence—I hope you do not think me
> prone to any iteration of nuptials—[31]

Her verbiage is so ponderously affected that even Waitwell is constrained to accept the challenge. Since Lady Wishfort is not aware
of the deception, however, he is perfectly safe in the facetious comment he makes in answer to her playful protests. It is one of the
most delicious tidbits in all Congreve:

> *Lady Wish.* If you think the least scruple of carnality was an
> ingredient—
> *Wait.* Dear madam, no. You are all camphor and frankincense,
> all chastity and odour.[32]

This discussion of ladies in the comedies of Congreve is intended to provide a fairly representative idea of Congreve's attitude toward them. He saves the satirical touch for the women who
are remembered for those follies which appear and reappear in society, especially affectation, which is ever present in the society of
the comedy of manners. In regard to the heroines, he is man enough
to admit his admiration for them, faults and all, and his weakness
where they are concerned. With this hint of resignation, he leaves

---

[30] IV, 1.
[31] IV, 2.
[32] IV, 2.

his depiction of women in the hands of the audience, indifferent about their reception of it. After all, he is not attempting a reformation of the feminine members of his class. The mere fact that his class had produced women like his Millamant and his Bracegirdle was enough for this man of the world who prided himself on his discrimination.

Congreve now turned his satirical powers into other channels, for, as he himself said, "there are but two sexes, male and female, men and women, which have a title to humanity; and if I leave one half of them out, the work will be imperfect."

In giving his impressions of men of society, Congreve had no such ideals as he had regarding women, unless this ideal were himself, for in these plays the men whom we are asked to admire resemble the type we are led to believe Congreve represented. He does not ridicule these men; if anything at all, his attitude toward them is a highly sympathetic one, for, being one of them, he realized how ludicrous was their assertion of supremacy in the social scale. His Bellmour, Mellefont, Valentine, and Mirabell are all "men" in the true sense of the word. While they have the vices common to all gentlemen of the Restoration, these vices do not make them despicable characters, but, paradoxically, enhance their attractiveness. Taking this for granted, Congreve chooses for his satire those men whose faults or idiosyncrasies make them noticeable among their fellowmen. To be sure, in his characterizations, Congreve often exaggerates their faults, but he does this only to make the audience a little self-conscious. In this way there is a possibility that the audience, in seeing itself thus mirrored, may correct its follies.

The examples selected to illustrate Congreve's satirical attitude in regard to men are those which linger long after the plays have been seen or read. Accordingly, we recall Heartwell, who is satirized for being a hypocrite; Fondlewife, for being a foolish old man; Witwoud, for being a pretender to wit; Captain Bluffe, for being the type of soldier ridiculed in comedy as early as the "Miles Gloriosus" of Plautus and the boastful Thraso of Terence (both of whom provided models for later creations such as Ralph Roister Doister, Lyly's Sir Tophas, Jonson's Bobadill, and Shakespeare's Falstaff); and, finally, Foresight, for being a superstitious dotard.

In George Heartwell, Congreve amusingly satirizes hypocrisy. The seriousness with which he denounces those temptations common to all mankind at once sets him apart as a rare bird. Unmarried men are always food for fun; but when a confirmed bachelor attempts to teach his friends how to act with regard to the other sex, there is material for satire. All his faults are excusable until he is actually caught indulging in those practices for which he censures others; then his sin is unpardonable, and he deserves all the punishment his friends choose to heap upon him. Weakness can be forgiven, but never hypocrisy. The humor in the case of Heartwell is that all are aware that he does not practice what he preaches; thus, the grander his denunciations and the bolder his polemics, the more ridiculous does he appear to the observer who is "in the know."

Congreve must have enjoyed creating this character, who is unconsciously doing a good job of "double-dealing" upon himself. Society is full of hypocrites, some more despicable than others, but the hypocritical bachelor is the sorriest figure of them all. He is criticizing actions and institutions which are perfectly natural and normal. His insistence that they are wrong is his grave fault.

If we should consider Heartwell's remarks as sincere, we might indeed marvel at a man of such strong convictions; but when we are aware of their emptiness, we must necessarily laugh out loud at him. His first speech of importance illustrates this point.

> *Heart.* I confess, you that are women's asses bear greater burdens; are forced to undergo dressing, dancing, singing, sighing, whining, rhyming, flattering, lying, grinning, cringing, and the drudgery of loving to boot.
> *Bell.* O brute! the drudgery of loving!
> *Heart.* Ay, why to come to love through all these encumbrances, is like coming to an estate overcharged with debts; which, by the time you have paid, yields no further profit than what the bare tillage and manuring of the land will produce at the expense of your own sweat.[33]

There is very little delicacy in the make-up of Heartwell, but he prided himself on not being a ladies' man, which fact, perhaps, partly exonerates his crudity. His misanthropy and his propensity for speaking the truth (which later are shown to be affected) remind one somewhat of Molière's Alceste, and arouse the suspicion that the French playwright had some influence upon Congreve, particularly when one takes into consideration likewise the later play, *The*

---

[33] *The Old Bachelor,* I, 1.

Way of the World. The moot question of foreign influence is not to be decided in this discussion, however, Alcestian though some of Heartwell's tendencies may appear to be on the surface.

By far the most amusing scene in which Heartwell appears is the following, which gives us in a very short time a good deal of insight into the character of this ultra-superficial bachelor. He has arrived at Silvia's house, and, unknown to him, has been followed all the way by Bellmour and Vainlove. He soliloquizes:

> *Heart.* Well, why do you not move? Feet, do your office—not one inch; no, foregad, I'm caught! There stands my north, and thither my needle points.—Now could I curse myself, yet cannot repent. O thou delicious, damned, dear, destructive woman! 'S death, how the young fellows will hoot me! I shall be the jest of the town. Nay, in two days I expect to be chronicled in ditty, and sung in woeful ballad, to the tune of "The Superannuated Maiden's Comfort," or "The Bachelor's Fall;" and upon the third I shall be hanged in effigy, pasted up for the exemplary ornament of necessary-houses and coblers' stalls. Death, I can't think on't!—I'll run into the danger to lose the apprehension. (*Enters Silvia's lodgings.*)
>
> *Bell.* A very certain remedy, *probatum est.*—Ha! ha! ha! poor George, thou art i' th' right, thou hast sold thyself to laughter; the ill-natured town will find the jest just where thou hast lost it. Ha! ha! how a' struggled, like an old lawyer between two fees![34]

This marks the beginning of the bachelor's fall, and from now on the satire is barbed and even cruel at times. Congreve lets his restraint go to the winds, and, as a result, depicts Heartwell in a most unfavorable light. The more he struggles and the lower he sinks into Silvia's net, the more amusing does the play become to the onlookers, and the audience is satisfied that he is getting his deserts. No one but Silvia could torment Heartwell in the way she does; being well versed in the technique, she finds it a simple matter to trap this gullible bachelor. The climax in the rise and fall of George Heartwell occurs when, his resistance entirely lost after one kiss at parting, he succumbs to her wiles and promises to marry her.

> *Heart.* I'm impatient till it be done; I will not give myself liberty to think, lest I should cool.—I will about a license straight; in the evening expect me.—One kiss more to confirm me mad; so. (*Exit.*)[35]

---

[34] III, 2.
[35] III, 4.

This from a man who has boasted vaingloriously of his sobriety
and strength of conviction where women are concerned! But the
unkindest cut of all is administered when Sharper purposely urges
Heartwell to come with him to Vainlove's "debauched" and "for-
saken" mistress, Silvia,—the lady with whom, but two hours earlier, Heartwell apparently had been joined in matrimony by a parson
who was really friend Bellmour in disguise! Poor George is panic-
stricken at the disclosal of the identity of Sharper's proposed bawd,
until, at his wits' end, he admits he is married, to the infinite amusement of Sharper.

> *Sharp.* My old bachelor married! that were a jest! ha! ha! ha!
> *Heart.* Death! d'ye mock me! Hark ye, if either you esteem my
> friendship or your own safety, come not near that house—that corner
> house—that hot brothel: ask no questions. (*Exit.*)
> *Sharp.* Mad, by this light!
>   Thus grief still treads upon the heels of pleasure;
>   Married in haste, we may repent at leisure.[36]

And after he has thus humbled himself in forgetting his pride for
passion, Silvia does just what one expects her to do—she jilts him
on their wedding day. In vain he rebukes Vainlove for his plight,
for, as he maintains, "If Silvia had not been your mistress, my wife
might have been honest."[37] At this point Heartwell is told the truth
about the deception practiced upon him, and he bears it all nobly.
No sooner does he find himself free again than he denounces women
and resolves to remain an old bachelor for the rest of his life. All
this merely emphasizes the extreme folly of being an old bachelor,
for the longer he remains single, the less wary and the more suscep-
tible does he become to that which he thinks he would most avoid.

When we have finished reading the play, we recall, not the successful love affairs therein, but the thwarted attempts of Heartwell,
who is destined to remain an old, gullible, and foolish bachelor. In
this satire of a bachelor's courtship, Congreve has managed to convey his opinion in regard to hypocrites, an opinion shared by the
general public.

The person who next merited the attention of the playwright
as he scanned the field for further victims is the stupid and insipid

---

[36] V, 3.
[37] V, 5.

Fondlewife. Like Captain Bluffe, he too is a stock character and
has appeared in scores of other plays with much success. Congreve
was thus certain of the reception Fondlewife would get and could
safely include him in this play, which is not particularly noteworthy
for originality of either plot or character. It is for the novel manner in which he handles these stage-worn stories and people that
Congreve deserves credit. Certainly, the jealous, superannuated
husband is no newcomer to the footlights, nor is this the last time
we are to meet him. Congreve may have been more directly influenced by another Restoration wit, Wycherley, and his characterization of Pinchwife, in *The Country Wife.* Sheridan, one of Congreve's best imitators, was influenced by Wycherley also, and carried over this same character into his *School for Scandal,* under the
name Sir Peter Teazle. Originality in this respect was not Sheridan's forte, as it was not the forte of Congreve, the literary predecessor in whose steps Sheridan was proud to follow.

The story of Fondlewife is that of the folly of the old man who
is conceited enough to believe he can make a young girl happy.
Chaucer, in his similar tale of January and May, deems it not conceit, but courage. According to Chaucer:

> ..., it is an heigh corage
> Of any man that stapen is in age
> To take a yong wyf; by my fader kyn,
> Youre herte hangeth on a joly pyn![38]

Courage or conceit, Fondlewife's predicament is one that is to be
expected from old age trying to persuade itself that youth is but
around the last corner, when, in reality, it is so far behind that it is
no longer visible, and that which old age thinks it sees is but a fig-
ment of the imagination. Fondlewife is just the opposite of Heartwell; he loves the fair sex and, old as he is, prefers marriage to
bachelordom, while Heartwell supposedly hates women and is loth
to surrender his freedom. Where Heartwell is a hypocrite, however, Fondlewife is a fool, pure and simple. Old enough to know
better, he was satisfied to run the risk of marrying the youthful
Laetitia, and the concern over her occasioned by his uncontrollable
jealousy is the subject for Congreve's satire. Laetitia is just old

---

[38] Robinson, F. N., *The Complete Works of Geoffrey Chaucer,* p. 142.

enough to see the humor in their ridiculous marriage, a fact which makes her husband all the more worried. Nor has she any scruples or qualms of conscience about cuckolding her aged spouse. Old Isaac's constant fear is that what tempted him will tempt others as well, and for this reason he is almost willing to forsake his business transactions in order to remain at home to keep guard over his "Cocky," as he playfully calls her. His parting admonitions to his wife on the subject of adultery and her firm denials of any such intentions on her part provide one of the most amusing scenes in the play. "Cocky" is so emphatic about her love for "Nykin," as she calls him, that Fondlewife determines to forfeit the five hundred pounds of his business deal to stay with her. This, however, is what she is farthest from desiring, and she slyly puts him off on another track—jealousy.

> *Laet.* No, you shan't neglect your business for me—no indeed
> you san't [*sic*], Nykin.—If you don't go, I'll think you been dealous
> of me still.
>   *Fond.* He! he! he! wilt thou, poor fool? then I will go, I won't
> be dealous.—Poor Cocky, kiss Nykin, kiss Nykin; ee! ee! ee!—Here
> will be the good man [Parson Spintext] anon, to talk to Cocky, and
> teach her how a wife ought to behave herself.[39]

Having arranged for Parson Spintext to keep "Cocky" from being lonesome, old "Nykin" feels a little better about thus leaving her, for in his opinion a parson is a man to be trusted with one's valuables. He departs, only to return unexpectedly just as Laetitia and the parson, who turns out to be Bellmour in disguise, are getting acquainted with each other. Fondlewife has come back for some papers which are in his wife's room; this development upsets her considerably, for, as it happens, Bellmour is ensconced in her bed, feigning a convulsive fit. The extraordinary thing about Fondlewife is his utter credulity in regard to what his wife tells him. He even believes her story about the parson, and all would be well if he did not accidentally spy Mr. Spintext's "prayer-book," which happens to be "The Innocent Adultery." It is only then that old "Nykin" is truly aroused to the extent that he rebukes his darling "Cocky."

---

[39] *The Old Bachelor,* IV, 2.

Laet. Dear husband, I'm amazed.—Sure it is a good book, and only tends to the speculation of sin.
Fond. Speculation! no, no; something went farther than speculation when I was not to be let in.—Where is this apocryphal elder? I'll ferret him. (*Exit.*)[40]

"Nykin" is now in a rage, for all his forebodings have come true, and Laetitia is Delilah, Magdalen, and Jezebel, all in one to him. Bellmour, seeing his cue, steps forth and tells the truth of his intentions, positively fascinating Fondlewife with his straightforwardness and thereby persuading him that his wife is innocent. The old dotard, anxious to be so convinced, finally yields to them. All is as before, and the mistakes of the night are forgiven and forgotten by Fondlewife in his endeavor to merit the affection of his young, beautiful, and wayward wife.

This completes Congreve's caricature of the old man who must perforce tie himself in matrimony to a young girl, and who is destined to spend the rest of his days, whether at home or abroad, worrying about her. He is a serious problem to himself, a bore and a nuisance to his wife, and a huge joke to his acquaintances. He is, nevertheless, a permanent fixture in society, which would be a great deal duller were the Fondlewifes and Laetitias absent from its midst.

Congreve protested that his audience was too hasty in its judgment "to distinguish betwixt the character of a Witwoud and a Truewit."[41] He had a genuine admiration for men of real wit and intellect. Nothing pleased him more than the repartee of clever people, and he himself was a master of the art of keeping the ball of conversation always swiftly moving back and forth. Nothing pleased him less, however, than the misbegotten attempts of the would-be wits to ape the natural and easy hits of the true-wits, for wits, like poets, are born, not made. Thus we have Witwoud, the representative of that class which Congreve despised. Every tavern had its share of these witlings who thought that the mere utterance of a simile, be it ever so trite, entitled them to membership in the select society of wits. Perhaps the reason why Congreve's audience could not distinguish between the two types is to be found

---

[40] IV, 6.
[41] Dedication of *The Way of the World*.

in the fact that there are always a great many more would-be wits than true-wits in every society, and, accordingly, the caricature is not readily recognized as such.

This satire, more than any other, perhaps, carries with it an air of utter disgust which subtly envelopes the character. It is evident that Congreve scorned this made-to-order wit, and for this reason represented Witwoud in as unfavorable a light as possible. His craftsmanship is evident in his method of delineation, for the audience is made to feel the Congrevean contempt not so much in the actual words or actions of the man in question, as in the shades and tones in which they appear. This filling in of the colors is often done by means of the comments of the other characters in response to Witwoud's remarks, as on the occasion when he informs his friends of the arrival of "the fool my brother."

> *Mir.* A fool, and your brother, Witwoud!
> *Wit.* Ay, ay, my half brother. My half brother he is, no nearer upon honour.
> *Mir.* Then 'tis possible he may be but half a fool.[42]

This is exactly the retort one might expect from Mirabell, who never misses a cue for a bright sally, particularly when it is at the expense of a Witwoud. The greatest weakness of these would-be wits, moreover, is their presumption that conversation of this type is welcomed by the Mirabells. Witwoud is little more than wit in its most primitive state, and the audience realizes that with him it will probably never rise much higher. An ironical note is touched in the speech wherein Witwoud characterizes his friend Petulant as having "a pretty deal of an odd sort of a small wit,"[43] and beseeches his listeners to be tolerant toward Petulant. This from one of the smallest wits indeed! Petulant's conversation is sprinkled with falsehoods as liberally as Witwoud's is garnished with similes; it is not always easy, accordingly, to decide which monotony is the more easily endured.

The scene which heralds the appearance of Millamant, in "full sail, with her fan spread and her streamers out, and a shoal of fools

---

[42] *The Way of the World*, I, 2.
[43] I, 2.

for tenders," is an extremely quotable one, for Witwoud is one of the fools and here is at his best.

> *Mir.* [*To Mrs. Millamant*] You seem to be unattended, madam— you used to have the *beau monde* throng after you; and a flock of gay fine perukes hovering round you.
> *Wit.* Like moths about a candle.—I had like to have lost my comparison for want of breath.
> *Mrs. Mil.* O I have denied myself airs to-day, I have walked as fast through the crowd.
> *Wit.* As a favourite just disgraced; and with as few followers.
> *Mrs. Mil.* Dear Mr. Witwoud, truce with your similitudes; for I'm as sick of 'em—
> *Wit.* As a physician of a good air.—I cannot help it, madam, though 'tis against myself.[44]

This is a sample of what goes on whenever Witwoud is encountered; and though at first this may prove fairly amusing, Congreve sees to it that the amusement is short-lived, and he makes Witwoud more and more objectionable. Nothing betrays Witwoud's ignorance more than the frigid welcome he bestows upon his brother, putting off recognition as long as possible by maintaining that " 'tis not modish to know relations in town,"[45] although even his brother knows better than to credit such an alibi. In creating the character of Witwoud, Congreve no doubt derived a great measure of satisfaction which in real life he could never have realized. He was, above all, a gentleman; therefore, his attitude toward the Witwouds was one of mere tolerance. It hurt him to listen to the makeshift attempts at wit and humor running amuck in society, and this caricature seemed the convenient method of retaliation.

In Captain Bluffe we find the Restoration version of the military braggart. He is one of the most familiar creations of the stage, and one with whom the audience is ever loth to part. His combined seriousness, boastfulness, and cowardice produce a character whose very contradictions render him highly amusing entertainment and excellent comic relief. There is no suspense in regard to Captain Bluffe, for, as is often true in Congreve's plays, the audience is prepared for him in the first scene of the play through the conver-

---

[44] II, 2.
[45] III, 2.

sation of Bellmour and Sharper, who are discussing Sir Joseph
Wittol and his adored champion—Bluffe.

> *Sharp.* Is that bully of his [Wittol's] in the army?
> *Bell.* No, but is a pretender, and wears the habit of a soldier;
> which now-a-days as often cloaks cowardice, as a black gown does
> atheism. . . . Speaks miracles, is the drum to his own praise—the
> only implement of a soldier he resembles; like that, being full of
> blustering noise and emptiness.
> *Sharp.* And like that, of no use but to be beaten.[46]

Here we have an idea of his current social reputation. Sir Joseph
Wittol's opinion of him is entirely different, however. So dependent
is he upon Bluffe that he refers to him as his "back," because "he
sticks as close to me."[47] With Bluffe behind him, Sir Joseph is, in
fact, almost brave, for, as his "back" reminds him : "He that knows
me must be a stranger to fear."[48] The grandiose airs, however, are
not sufficient to hide the false front. Bluffe's bravery vanishes into
nothingness when a test demanding real courage occurs. His assumed attitude of modesty is as ridiculous as the rest of his make-up,
for he monopolizes the conversation by constant allusion to it. His
manner of talking is one that encourages questions on the part of
his audience ; then, abetted and prompted by his witling admirer, he
is ready to continue with his fabrications. Sir Joseph is content
with basking in some of Bluffe's reflected glory. Thus, when Bluffe
is modestly proclaiming the important part he played in the wars,
he is assisted by Sir Joseph :

> *Sir Jo.* Ay, this damned modesty of yours—egad, if he would put
> in for't he might be made general himself yet.
> *Bluffe.* O fy, no, Sir Joseph!—you know I hate this.

He goes on to boast of his sword.

> *Bluffe.* This sword, I think, I was telling you of, Mr. Sharper,—
> this sword—I'll maintain to be the best divine, anatomist, lawyer,
> or casuist in Europe; it shall decide a controversy or split a cause.
> *Sir Jo.* Nay, now I must speak; it will split a hair, by the Lord
> Harry, I have seen it.

---

[46] *The Old Bachelor,* I, 1.
[47] II, 1.
[48] II, 1.

> *Bluffe.* Zounds, sir, it's a lie! you have not seen it, nor shan't
> see it; sir, I say you can't see; what d'ye say to that now?
> *Sir Jo.* I am blind.[49]

Poor Sir Joseph is completely crushed by the wrath of his idol, for
Bluffe is a bully toward anyone weaker than himself. When he is
berated and kicked by Sharper and Bellmour, Bluffe takes it all
without a word, to the amazement of Sir Joseph. Not until the
adversaries have departed from the scene does he draw his sword
and work himself up into a belated rage. To his "I'll die before I'll
suffer it," Sir Joseph counters with entreaties:

> *Sir Jo.* (*Aside.*) O Lord, his anger was not raised before!—
> (*Aloud.*) Nay, dear captain, don't be in a passion now he's gone.—
> Put up, put up, dear back, 'tis your Sir Joseph begs; come, let me
> kiss thee; so, so, put up, put up.

And Bluffe, of course, complies after slight coaxing, insisting,
"Well, Sir Joseph, at your entreaty...."[50]

The final touch, when Bluffe and Sir Joseph are hoodwinked
into marrying Silvia and Lucy on the assumption that the ladies are
Araminta and Belinda, is an amusing one, since even these entangle-
ments are better than the two deserve.

Captain Bluffe and his faithful dog, Sir Joseph, are merely the
Plautian "Miles Gloriosus" and the parasite, slightly retouched and
brought up to date, but retaining all their original follies.

Like comic-satirists in general, Congreve was advanced for the
age in which he happened to live, and had no scruples about ridiculing and breaking down some of the favorite illusions of his world.
One of these illusions was the current faith in astrology. It was a
day when the foremost and, presumably, most enlightened men
and women indulged in this pseudo science to such an extent that it
became more or less of a vice with them. Horoscopes were assidu-
ously read and their prognostications faithfully followed Congreve was clearsighted enough to see the folly arising from this
delusion, and, no doubt, was looked upon as a rebel by his compatri
ots. In *Love for Love* he availed himself of the opportunity for

---

[49] II, 1.
[50] III, 3.

some playful banter at the expense of this superstitious cult, and
the result was the character of Foresight, at once recognizable as a
cartoon.

Foresight's life is run according to the best astrological pre-
cepts. He himself thrives on omens and can not understand why
the other members of his family do not follow his example. Like
Fondlewife, he too is jealous of his young and handsome wife, but,
unlike the former, Foresight explains his torments as the "will of
the stars." He is pleased with himself when he puts on one stock-
ing on the wrong side and steps out of bed backwards, for these are
good omens. He will see Sir Sampson at three o'clock because it is
a good hour for business, governed as it is by Mercury. He forbids
Angelica to leave the house because the absence of all the women
forebodes mischief to the head of the house. How easily he is pro-
voked by Sir Sampson, who in jest ventures to doubt "that celes-
tial science." The heated dialogue that ensues is reminiscent of
that between Hotspur and Glendower when the latter boasts of his
supernatural accomplishments. When Foresight proclaims his
astrological knowledge, he is countered by even greater boasts on
the part of Sir Sampson, who claims to "know the length of the
Emperor of China's foot; have kissed the Great Mogul's slipper,
and rid a hunting upon an elephant with the Cham of Tartary."[51]
Foresight is so deeply hurt by this that he is ready to call off his
daughter's marriage to Sir Sampson's son until he is finally convinced that it was all in fun.

Foresight is made extremely ridiculous by his excessive gullibility, occasioned no doubt by his preoccupation with other than
earthly affairs. One of the most amusing scenes in the play is that
in which Foresight is persuaded by Scandal that he is ill and allows
himself to be sent to bed, thus leaving the way clear for Scandal to
spend the night with Mrs. Foresight.

Another person to impose on Foresight's credulity is Valentine,
who in his feigned madness carries on a conversation which causes
his father to exclaim: "Body o' me, he talks sensibly in his madness!
has he no intervals?" Foresight, however, is very gentle with Valentine, for he reverences "a man whom the vulgar think mad," and
whose "sayings are very mysterious and hieroglyphical."[52]

---

[51] *Love for Love,* II, 1.
[52] IV, 3.

Foresight represents the type of satire Congreve employed when he was merely amused. There is no cynicism to be found in this caricature of the deluded astrologer, for Congreve did not actually harbor malice toward the believers. The absurdness of their implicit belief is what entertained him, and he took this means of transmitting to his audience some idea of the fun he derived from the criticism.

Although Congreve has given a great share of his attention to writing about men, he has allotted a greater proportion to women. Women played a very important part in Restoration society and particularly in the circle in which Congreve moved. Guessing at his character from the information one gleans from biographical sources and from his writings, one might venture to say that Congreve was not the man to participate in all those phases of the social life he described, but rather was content to sit on the sidelines and there gather his testimony and his experience. Perhaps his gout impeded his activity. There is no doubt, however, that women held a great attraction for him and presented fascinating material for him to study. Therein may be found the reason why, when he chose to write, he found the satire of women to provide a more extensive hunting-ground than that of his own sex. In summing up the results, one must admit that he has, as he intended, given a fairly inclusive picture of humanity, having omitted neither one of the two sexes.

Let us now observe Congreve's treatment of the conventional institutions—love, marriage, children—with which society is commonly concerned.

The question of Congreve's satire on love has already been dealt with incidentally, for the discussion of his attitude toward men and women, of necessity, involves some consideration of his views regarding love. The men and women of the Restoration prided themselves on the almost brutal coldness with which they looked upon love and marriage; but Congreve, coming so late in the period, delved beneath the brittle exterior affected by the coquette and the fop, and found there all the original warmth and emotion ordinarily associated with love. He, in turn, transferred his findings to the stage, and presented a type of Restoration love far different from the carnal affection or the purely intellectualized variety displayed in the majority of plays of this period. He gives us people swayed

by love's passions, contending against the forces of human nature.
There is also beauty and poetry in this love, for the aesthetic side
of the playwright's nature could conceive of it in no other way.
True love was sacred to Congreve, and it was never satirized. The
only touch of satire to be found in this connection is his reflection on
the plight of the victims, particularly the men. False love, however, Congreve vigorously assailed, for, despising pretension in general, he protested at the defamation of what seemed to him one of
life's greatest and most beautiful ideals. He criticized the women
for their denials of love, and he mocked the men for allowing themselves to be treated as mere pawns in the game. He ridiculed the
old who fancied they were still young, and he made fun of the young
who imagined they were too sophisticated to bother with love's trivialities.

In the Restoration period, matrimony was an institution which
was generally ridiculed in the world of society. In an age when in-
decorous living and indiscreet love was the rule, there was no need
for marriage, except as a convenience. We have the current philosophy of marriage voiced by Mirabell when he reminds his former
mistress, Mrs. Fainall:

> *Mir.* Why do we daily commit disagreeable and dangerous ac-
> tions? to save that idol, reputation. If the familiarities of our loves
> had produced that consequence of which you were apprehensive,
> where could you have fixed a father's name with credit, but on a hus-
> band?...A better man than Fainall ought not to have been sacri-
> ficed to the occasion; a worse had not answered to the purpose. When
> you are weary of him you know your remedy.[53]

This was the accepted opinion of the day. Congreve seems to have
seen something more worth while in marriage, for even his most
inaccessible hero and heroine are made to yield to it eventually.
Perhaps there was much of the conservative in the playwright,
which came to light in his criticism of the manners of the society
with which he was affiliated. At least one can assume that he advocates marriage, for he leads all his favorite characters into it finally,
although he reserves this conclusion only for the true lovers.

In regard to the marriages of convenience, Congreve expresses
his disdain in the words of Heartwell, who scoffs at the suggestion

---

[53] *The Way of the World,* II, 2.

of creating a family and providing for children. We hear the disapproval of the playwright who fears his ideals are in danger of being shattered by the iconoclasts who insist on making a mockery of marriage. That he has his doubts on the subject, however, is evinced in the conversation of Cynthia and Mellefont. It is as if Congreve were debating the question with himself, yet always coming back to his original opinion.

> *Cyn.* I'm thinking, though marriage makes man and wife one flesh, it leaves them still two fools; and they become more conspicuous by setting off one another.
> *Mel.* That's only when two fools meet, and their follies are opposed.
> *Cyn.* Nay, I have known two wits meet, and by the opposition of their wit render themselves as ridiculous as fools....[54]

Congreve's final decision is expressed by Mellefont:

> *Mel.* No, marriage is rather like a game at bowls; Fortune indeed makes the match, and the two nearest, and sometimes the two farthest, are together; but the game depends entirely upon judgment.[55]

Above all, Congreve insisted on the sincerity of both parties concerned. He objected to the casualness with which marriage was regarded by the Mrs. Frails and the Witwouds. An instance of this careless attitude is presented by Witwoud, who, in a supposedly unguarded moment, inquires:

> *Wit.* ...Fainall, how does your lady? Gad, I say anything in the world to get this fellow [his half brother] out of my head. I beg pardon that I should ask a man of pleasure, and the town, a question at once so foreign and domestic....[56]

And in the superb scene in which Millamant lays down the law to Mirabell, we see the end of Congreve's quibbling with himself, for he has made them give in at last to the prospects of wedded bliss.

With children Congreve and Restoration society had little to do. At odd moments they appear suddenly on the scene to the amazement of their parents, and they are as quickly dismissed.

---

[54] *The Double-Dealer,* II, 1.
[55] II, 1.
[56] *The Way of the World,* I, 2.

Lady Froth is the only one who actually boasts of her offspring, little Sappho. Valentine is genuinely taken aback when confronted by his illegitimate son. Jeremy, his servant, announces that "there's your father's steward, and the nurse with one of your children from Twitnam," to which Valentine replies: "Pox on her! could she find no other time to fling my sins in my face? Here, give her this (*Gives money*), and bid her trouble me no more;..."[57] But this is expected of the Restoration gallant, for children are mere incidents in the life he leads.

As for religion, Jeremy Collier, attacking Congreve in his *Short View of the Immorality and Profaneness of the English Stage,* accused him of dealing too lightly with sacred subjects. For his examples he cited trifles such as that in *The Old Bachelor,* where a parson is referred to as "Mr. Prig," and that in *The Double-Dealer,* where Lady Plyant speaks of "Jehu," her hackney-coachman. On such flimsy grounds did the militant clergyman base his assertion that Congreve and the rest of his tribe were guilty of sins against religion. Collier upheld the old idea of the unassailability of anyone or anything connected with the church or religion in general. Congreve, on the other hand, saw no reason why members of the cloth should be immune to criticism, particularly when their conduct justified it.

In *The Old Bachelor* the satire is to be found in Fondlewife's inviting Tribulation Spintext to stay with his wife while he goes away on business. It is his conviction that all parsons are models of piety that affords amusement. According to Collier, even Congreve's disguising the rake Bellmour in the "fanatic habit" was sacrilegious, but to Congreve it was merely furthering the jest. Collier might as well have criticized Congreve's allowing Fondlewife to call his wife "Jezebel," as his letting Lady Plyant have a coachman named "Jehu," Jezebel being as much a Biblical allusion as the "Jehu" to which he called attention.

Occasionally Congreve does insert a satirical bit at the expense of the clergy. Lucy, the maid, on being kissed by the disguised Bellmour, remarks, "O Lard! I believe you are a parson in good earnest, you kiss so devoutly."[58] There is also satire in the description of the parson's apparel, as offered by Setter:

---

[57] *Love for Love,* I, 2.
[58] *The Old Bachelor,* V, 1.

> *Set.* All, all, sir; the large sanctified hat, and the little precise band, and a swinging long spiritual cloak, to cover carnal knavery— not forgetting the black patch, which Tribulation Spintext wears, as I'm informed, upon one eye, as a penal mourning for the ogling offences of his youth; and some say, with that eye he first discovered the frailty of his wife.[59]

And in Bellmour's observation:

> *Bell.* I wonder why all our young fellows should glory in an opinion of atheism, when they may be so much more conveniently lewd under the coverlet of religion.[60]

In *The Double-Dealer* Congreve presents another caricature of a parson in Mr. Saygrace, Maskwell's "little Levite." As Maskwell says, "There is no plot, public or private, that can expect to prosper without one of them has a finger in't."[61] In *Love for Love* Congreve was too preoccupied to bother with the religious; he had more interesting subjects which demanded his attention. When he presented *The Way of the World,* he took special pains to avoid any reflection on religion, for he was just recuperating from his unsuccessful bout with Collier, and he now left well enough alone. Lady Wishfort, however, is permitted to suggest *The Short View of the Stage* to entertain Mrs. Marwood while she herself dresses.

One can not deny that Congreve satirized religion and the clergy, but, proportionally, this satire comprises an inconspicuous part of his work and is generally thrown in with the rest as incidental humor for good measure. It is obvious that Congreve's slurs were not in the least harmful, and for this reason Collier seems to have been unjustified in attacking Congreve on this count. Such is the fate of the satirist, unfortunately; if he is given to criticism, he must expect it in return. Congreve, however, was not accustomed to such treatment and resented the infringement on his private authority.

The simplicity of the country and of its people always has provided occasion for satire, and Congreve likewise took advantage of it. It is difficult to believe that Congreve, metropolitan though he was, ignored the natural beauty of the country. At least he was

---

[59] III, 2.
[60] IV, 1.
[61] *The Double-Dealer,* V, 3.

consistent in satirizing, not the beauties of nature, but the people who emerge, awkward and crude, from such backgrounds.

The first caricature of country folk appears early in *The Old Bachelor* and is presented breathlessly by Belinda. Her description of the "country squire, with the equipage of a wife and two daughters," is not very complimentary, and she says of the girls:

> *Belin.* Ay, o' my conscience, fat as barn-door fowl; but so bedecked, you would have taken 'em for Friesland hens, with their feathers growing the wrong way.—O, such outlandish creatures! Such Tramontanae, and foreigners to the fashion, or anything in practice! I had not patience to behold—I undertook the modelling of one of their fronts, the more modern structure.[62]

Belinda can scarcely restrain her laughter when she relates how the girl gave her "two apples, piping hot, out of her under-petticoat pocket" in return for her assistance. The other, she fancies, was "like the front of her father's hall; her eyes were the two jut-windows, and her mouth the great door, most hospitably kept open for the entertainment of travelling flies."[63] One can imagine how awkward they must have been from Belinda's report that they tore two pairs of kid gloves in the mere process of trying them on.

In *Love for Love* Congreve gives his audience a complete picture of the country hoyden, in the character of Prue, who has been transplanted in the city for a proposed marriage with sailor Ben, Valentine's brother. Unfortunately, she meets Tattle first, and is completely taken in by his attentions. The scene in which he instructs Prue in the gentle art of love-making is a very entertaining one. Its boisterous style is reminiscent of Wycherley; its characters call to mind Farquhar's Cherry and Archer. The same risqué note that we find in Wycherley is achieved here, likewise, by means of the double entendres, and the repartee has the same celerity found in the give-and-take of Cherry and Archer. Prue, however, lacks the smartness of Cherry, and instead is gifted with a talent for learning quickly. Even Tattle is forced to admit that "that was as well as if you had been born and bred in Covent Garden,"[64] though one naturally questions his sincerity. Having tasted of the foppish ways of Tattle and taking it for granted that he returns her affection, she

---

[62] *The Old Bachelor*, IV, 4.
[63] IV, 4.

has no use whatsoever for the seafaring Ben. Essentially, Prue and Ben have many characteristics in common, for both have grown up in an environment which encourages frankness and naturalness. Ben's decision in regard to Prue is that it is "more fitting for her to learn her sampler and make dirt-pies, than to look after a husband."[65] The misled girl gets her first experience of the double-dealing ways of city life when, having obtained her father's consent to marry Tattle, she is brushed aside. All efforts to console her are in vain, for Prue has been fascinated by Tattle's manners. Her disappointment is so great that she threatens to marry Robin the butler, so eager is she to have a husband.

This is Congreve's satirical conception of the awkward country cousin, who, in attempting to ape the city madams, merely succeeds in making a fool of herself. Prue might be attractive in her own rural sphere in the midst of the swains and damsels who are strangers to the sophistries of the town. She is unfortunate, however, in having obtained this glimpse of the metropolis, for now she can be happy neither in the city nor in the country.

For a "take-off" on the country male, Congreve has given us Sir Wilfull, the half-brother of the conceited Witwoud discussed earlier. Sir Wilfull is an extreme example of nature in the rough. He possesses all the undesirable qualities that one associates with the outlandish yokel and few desirable ones. He is uncouth in manners and language, unkempt in appearance, and uneducated in the ways of society. His sense of humor is coarse and offensive, while his outspokenness, bordering on insolence, is generally out of turn, particularly among new acquaintances. He has stopped in London to visit his brother before setting out on his travels on the continent, and one can visualize the type of traveller this awkward fellow will make. He is to be admired for his sincerity, which is in such decided contrast to the affectation of the Londoners; but his actions are such that his relatives are constantly apologizing for his lack of breeding. For example, when the maid announces to Lady Wishfort that "dinner is impatient," Wilfull's undisguised country appetite is at once aroused:

---

[64] *Love for Love,* II, 2.
[65] IV, 3.

    Sir Wil. Impatient! Why then belike it won't stay till I pull off my boots.—Sweetheart, can you help me to a pair of slippers?— My man's with his horses, I warrant. .

    Lady Wish. Fy, fy, nephew! you would not pull off your boots here?—Go down into the hall—dinner shall stay for you.—My nephew's a little unbred....[66]

The most amusing feature in this caricature is his aunt's design to marry him to Millamant. A more incongruous juxtaposition of characters could not have been evolved than that of Millamant and Sir Wilfull, who are as different from each other as the two poles. Knowing from the start that Congreve has something better in store for the heroine, one does not take Wilfull's intentions very serious- ly. When he has his first encounter with Millamant, the rustic boldness of the country fellow gives way to a genuine awe in the presence of such beauty and sophistication. He has, of course, lost his case even before attempting to woo the lady, but, to make his defeat more final, he displays his lack of education the moment he steps upon her threshold. She is repeating to herself lines from "natural, easy Suckling," and Wilfull, thinking she is addressing him, counters with: "Anan? Suckling! no such suckling neither, cousin, nor stripling: I thank Heaven, I'm no minor."[67] He is ig- norant of the fact that Millamant is tolerating him for the moment while she awaits a visit from Mirabell. He is also unaware that his friends and relatives are tolerating him in anticipation of his setting off on his travels. He is, nevertheless, something of a hero when he gives up Millamant to Mirabell in the realization that they are best suited for each other.

Both Prue and Sir Wilfull are exaggerated characters, but this is to be expected in satire, which makes the worst features of the caricature stand out prominently while the redeeming qualities are obscured. Congreve's opinion of the country and its people is not a high one, and his contemptuous attitude was shared by all the London smart set. In this way he expresses his urbanity and that of his clique.

Congreve occasionally gives attention to education. He was well aware of the futility of learning when one is fighting poverty. Although he himself was never in such dire straits, he could sym-

---

[66] *The Way of the World,* III, 3.
[67] IV, 1.

pathize with the literati who were. His defense of the indigent scholars expressed itself in satire on the unequal apportionment of talents and riches. Valentine tries to exist by means of his books, but Jeremy, his man, is not satisfied with this literary fare. Almost at the point of starvation, Valentine advises Jeremy:

> *Val.* Read, read, sirrah! and refine your appetite; learn to live upon instruction; feast your mind, and mortify your flesh; read, and take your nourishment in at your eyes; shut up your mouth, and chew the cud of understanding; so Epictetus advises.

Jeremy is not impressed by this admonition and, in the layman's jargon, replies:

> *Jer.* Sir, you're a gentleman, and probably understand this fine feeding; but if you please, I had rather be at board-wages. Does your Epictetus, or your Seneca here, or any of these poor rich rogues, teach you how to pay your debts without money? Will they shut up the mouths of your creditors? Will Plato be bail for you? or Diogenes, because he understands confinement, and lived in a tub, go to prison for you? 'S life, sir, what do you mean? to mew yourself up here with three or four musty books, in commendation of starving and poverty?[68]

Congreve continues on the same theme a little later when the would-be wit, Tattle, is considering enlisting Jeremy in his service, and is reviewing Jeremy's qualifications.

> *Jer.* Sir, I have the seeds of rhetoric and oratory in my head; I have been at Cambridge.
> *Tat.* Ay! 'tis well enough for a servant to be bred at a university: but the education is a little too pedantic for a gentleman....[69]

The implication of the satire is obvious, for the would-be wits were pretenders to education as well as to wit.

The other outstanding satire on such pretensions is in the character of Lady Froth, who, as we have already seen, affects a knowledge of literature and conceitedly thinks she is writing "an heroic poem" on her husband's love. She tries always to use long words and to intersperse them with quotations from the French as a mark

---

[68] *Love for Love,* I, 1.
[69] V, 2.

of her broad education, but, unfortunately, she can think of nothing less trite than "bel air" and "je ne sais quoi."

To Congreve, people like Tattle and Lady Froth seemed to exist simply for contrast with the wits, and they were to be tolerated if possible. They detracted so much from the pleasantness of the society he loved, however, that he could not forego criticism of them whenever an opportunity presented itself.

Congreve turned away from the stage and gave up the business of being a poet, partly because his independent spirit would not permit him to sue indefinitely for the patronage upon which poets depended at the time. All too frequently the patrons themselves were but poetasters who presumed to dictate to writers who possessed real talent but lacked the financial means and influence for individual exhibition. Congreve realized how transient is fame, particularly so when unabetted by the necessary support of some nobleman. He was, moreover, annoyed by the unwarranted assumption of superiority in the attitude of society toward the poet. The reception commonly accorded the comic poet, or playwright, was so cool that even the ideal of "art for art's sake" did not always provide sufficient consolation. For this reason, Congreve saw fit to include some lines illustrating and criticizing this hostility. Valentine, in his poverty, threatens to write a play, and Jeremy, horrified, warns him of the disadvantages attendant upon the profession and the low esteem in which it is held. Even Jeremy feels he will be losing dignity by remaining in the service of a playwright, for, as he says, "You're undone, sir, you're ruined, you won't have a friend left in the world if you turn poet."[70] Scandal arrives, and he too sides with Jeremy in expressing public opinion:

> *Scan.* Poet! he shall turn soldier first, and rather depend upon the outside of his head than the lining. Why, what the devil! has not your poverty made you enemies enough? must you needs show your wit to get more?...No, turn pimp, flatterer, quack, lawyer, parson, be chaplain to an atheist, or stallion to an old woman, anything but poet; a modern poet is worse, more servile, timorous and fawning, than any I have named....[71]

---

[70] I, 1.
[71] I, 1.

Valentine is finally persuaded to give up such a rash ambition.

Before leaving the subject of playwrights and plays, however, Congreve scores another satirical touch upon the Restoration audience. He was entirely out of sympathy with the fops who came to the theatre merely to show off their clothes, their women, their wit, and, by their inattention to the creation of the poet, their ignorance as well. Thus, in *The Double-Dealer* Lord Froth holds forth on the drama in reply to the questions of Mellefont and Careless.

> *Mel.* But does your lordship never see comedies?
> *Lord Froth.* O yes, sometimes;—but I never laugh.
> *Mel.* No!
> *Lord Froth.* O no;—never laugh indeed, sir.
> *Care.* No! why, what d'ye go there for?
> *Lord Froth.* To distinguish myself from the commonalty, and mortify the poets: the fellows grow so conceited when any of their foolish wit prevails upon the side-boxes,—I swear—he! he! he! I have often constrained my inclination to laugh,—he! he! he! to avoid giving them encouragement.[72]

With such perverse theatre-goers, it is not to be wondered at that Congreve left them for the more appreciative audience to be found among the true wits of the smart set.

---

[72] *The Double-Dealer,* I, 2.

CHAPTER II

RICHARD BRINSLEY BUTLER SHERIDAN

Close upon the heels of Congreve in the history of the comedy of manners comes Sheridan,[1] akin to him in both substance and spirit. Congreve, born in England, passed his childhood and youth in Ireland; as if to even up matters for the students of English literature, Sheridan, born in Ireland, spent his early years in England. Thus, both men had or soon acquired a generous share of the Irish comic spirit. Like Congreve, Sheridan was of a well-known family, though he was not born to the purple. It was for the most part through his own untiring efforts and charming personality that he was admitted to aristocratic circles. His father, after a rather successful dramatic career, retired from the stage to become a teacher of elocution. Later he won recognition for compiling his *General Dictionary of the English Language*. Sheridan's mother was a novelist and playwright of some note, one of whose plays, *The Discovery*, was acted by David Garrick. With such a background of talent, Sheridan's successful career comes not as a surprise but as a matter of course. Clayton Hamilton says of him:

> He was a thoroughly conventional person. He did everything that was being done by the best people of his time; only, he took care to do each thing better than it could possibly be done by anybody else in England. It was, as I have said, a very simple formula.[2]

Sheridan was not so much interested in art for art's sake as in art for money's sake, for, we must remember, his play-writing career was occasioned by financial need after his sudden and romantic marriage to Elizabeth Linley, a professional singer of fame and beauty. His inherited knowledge of the theatre made him realize that the simplest way to achieve the best results was that of pleasing the audience. He had neither the time nor the temperament for creating original stories, and he employed plots which were as stock as the characters in them. He did, however, render them more

---

[1] The plays of Sheridan on which the discussion in this chapter is based are *The Rivals* (1775), *The School for Scandal* (1777), and *The Critic* (1779). The dates are those of presentation.

[2] Hamilton, Clayton, *Plays by Richard Brinsley Sheridan*, Introduction, p. xii.

lifelike by imparting to them the manners and speech of his contemporaries.

On the other hand, Sheridan managed to recapture the spirit
of the previous century in his presentation of heartless women,
scheming men, and, in general, a cold and worldly-wise society; he
tempered this, however, with a genuine warmth of tone decidedly
lacking in the more formal plays of Congreve. To satisfy the tastes
of an audience not yet recovered from the verbal lashing administered at the close of the previous century by the vehement Jeremy
Collier, and to appease his own desire to follow the dictates of society, Sheridan frequently seasoned his comedy with sentimentality,
that quality in which Georgians were wont to revel. Aware of the
hypocrisy of exaggerated sentimentality, he attacked it through the
medium of satire. The fact that comedy was deteriorating through
the continued use of this same sentimentality stimulated the young
Sheridan to call attention to the regrettable situation. As early as
the Prologue to *The Rivals,* Sheridan's intentions in this direction
are indicated, particularly when he laments that "the goddess of
the woful countenance—the sentimental Muse" threatens to dis-
place the Muse of comedy.

Unlike Congreve, who in his five acts found innumerable opportunities for satire, Sheridan lavishly utilized an entire play for
satirizing one quality or institution or person. Thus, *The Rivals* is
almost entirely given over to an exposé of hypocritical sentimentality; *The School for Scandal* is a thorough-going criticism of malicious scandal-mongering and of sentimentality; and *The Critic* is
a final belittling of not only the so-called "genteel comedy" but also
true comedy with a moral purpose. His admission in the Prologue
to *The Critic* clearly reflects Sheridan's attitude:

> Thalia, once so ill-behaved and rude,
> Reform'd, is now become an arrant prude;
> Retailing nightly to the yawning pit
> The purest morals, undefiled by wit!

Accordingly, Sheridan set about remedying the shortcomings apparent in the comic drama of the day, and thereby provided poster-
ity with caricatures whose significance is not impaired with the passing of years.

In literary wit Congreve is easily the superior of the two, but in simple, infectious gayety Sheridan surpasses his predecessor. Unlike Congreve, Sheridan had but one ambition, that of being a gentleman. Whatever he did was directed toward this end. When he married Elizabeth Linley, he turned to writing plays as the easiest way of earning money to support his young and beautiful wife. Lucrative as it was, such a livelihood did not satisfy him for long, and a little over four years after his first success Sheridan deserted the drama for politics, in which field he was more certain to achieve the recognition he most desired.

Only once did he interrupt his dramatic inactivity. At the end of the century he adapted Kotzebue's tragedy *The Spaniards in Peru,* and presented his version of it, entitled *Pizarro,* in 1799. Although the popularity of *Pizarro* was considerable, it was not great enough to attract him again to his original profession.

The dramatic output of the second half of the eighteenth century was predominantly of the sentimental variety. Though occasionally plays appeared bearing resemblance to the earlier "manners" school, such examples were few and far between. Part of the blame for this situation is generally attributed to the French playwrights who were putting the finishing touches on their "comédie larmoyánte." But foreign models alone could not have exerted such influence on the drama, had not the British theatre turned sentimental of its own accord. This is not, however, the place to discuss the subject in detail, or to prove that the eighteenth century was indeed, as Nicoll terms it, "a weeping age."[3] By the time Sheridan appeared on the Georgian theatrical scene, the sentimentality of the period was no longer novel; it was taken for granted, not only by those who continued to indulge in it, but by those who criticized it as well. This was a fortunate thing for Sheridan, who chose to be a member of the critical faction.

The words "sentiment" and "sentimentality," although they are constantly being confused, are not synonymous. Sentiment is nothing more than the truthful expression of the feelings of a sensitive person; it is sincere and unaffected. Sentimentality is a self-conscious indulgence in feeling, having for its aim either the approval of one's self as a virtuous person (moral sentimentality)

---

[3] Nicoll, Allardyce, *XVIII Century Drama, 1750-1800,* p. 157.

or the mere pleasure in the feeling (romantic sentimentality). Moral sentimentality very often results in egotism, since the individual indulges in this moral sentimentality because he approves of himself as being a moral person. Romantic sentimentality is much pleasanter to behold, since it is generally motivated by a desire for fun or pleasure of any kind. Laurence Sterne's Yorick, in *A Sentimental Journey,* is far more tolerable than Richardson's Pamela or Fielding's Joseph Andrews.

In Sheridan's plays the characters most easily remembered for their indulgence in sentimentality are Lydia Languish, Julia, and Faulkland, in *The Rivals;* and Joseph Surface and Maria, in *The School for Scandal.* Faulkland and Surface are obvious satires on the affected, virtuous strain. Julia and Maria, however, must have awed many a female of a generation brought up on that "genteel comedy" which Goldsmith derided and sought to remedy. Yet, failing to recognize the ridicule in the sustained virtues of Julia and Maria, such an audience could not but detect the satirical elements in Lydia's romantic capriciousness, in Faulkland's everlasting morality and his doubting of Julia's love, and in Joseph Surface's hypocritical sentimentality.

In dealing first with the romantic aspect of sentimentality, we shall need to glance at one of Sheridan's dramatic devices. In introducing the important characters, Sheridan again and again makes use of that ancient and well-worn device of putting the descriptions into the mouths of minor players. Congreve's technique of introduction, though similar, is not quite so obvious. Since the audience never anticipate the subtler artistry of Congreve, they can the more readily forgive Sheridan's undisguised methods. Sheridan is too much preoccupied with the matter of getting on with the plot to bother with such trivialities, and, accordingly, takes advantage of the easiest method of presentation. Thus, the conversation of the servants introduces us to the first of his satirical characterizations, Lydia Languish (whose surname Sheridan lifted from Congreve's *The Way of the World*). Confiding to Thomas, Fag at once reveals the nature of Lydia's idiosyncrasy:

> *Fag.* Ah! Thomas, there lies the mystery o' the matter. Hark 'ee, Thomas, my master is in love with a lady of a very singular taste: a lady who likes him better as a half pay ensign than if she knew he

was son and heir to Sir Anthony Absolute, a baronet of three thousand a year.[4]

When we actually come face to face with Lydia, we derive an immediate clue to her character from her literary tastes, which incline to such current fiction as *The Delicate Distress, Peregrine Pickle, Humphrey Clinker,* and *A Sentimental Journey.* On her bookshelf is to be found likewise *The Innocent Adultery,* the damaging book in Bellmour's possession in *The Old Bachelor!* As we become better acquainted with this romantic young lady, we are almost ready to agree with Sir Anthony Absolute, who reflects on her misconduct: "ay, this comes of her reading!"[5]

Lydia Languish is a lively and likeable person even though she illustrates the eighteenth-century flair for sentimentality carried to the extreme. Is it, moreover, farfetched to venture a guess that he derived more than a mere suggestion for this characterization from the romantic lady he himself wooed and won? From her surreptitious reading Lydia has conjured up an impossible world of romance in which she and her loved one are the only inhabitants of any importance. She has given her imagination free rein, and the result is a curious combination of sentiment, vanity, love, and sheer caprice. She has no ulterior motive in carrying on these fanciful notions other than the mere pleasure she derives from doing so. The conventional mode of life is not for her, and in her craving for adventure she is so completely carried away by her romantic ideas that the result is a highly amusing caricature of a young woman of the eighteenth century.

An occasional passage indicates clearly Lydia's line of thought. Deliberately she quarrels with the man she loves for the sole reason that "as often as we had been together, we had never had a quarrel, and, somehow, I was afraid he would never give me an opportunity."[6] When Julia reminds Lydia of the latter's thirty thousand pounds, Lydia responds:

> *Lyd.* But you know I lose most of my fortune if I marry without my aunt's consent, till of age; and that is what I have determined to

---

[4] *The Rivals,* I, 1.

[5] I, 2.

[6] I, 2.

do, ever since I knew the penalty. Nor could I love the man, who
would wish to wait a day for the alternative.[7]

Some may argue that Lydia's perversities are devised by her merely
to shock her listeners. This is really not so. There is definite sincerity in her efforts to bring a little glamour into an otherwise drab
existence, but the satire is in the fact that she goes to the same extreme as her fellow Georgians in her romantic quest.

At no time, however, does her taste for the romantic deceive
her lover, Captain Absolute, who, to make his case stronger, has
disguised himself as Ensign Beverley. His convictions on the subject are noteworthy:

> Softly, softly; for though I am convinced my little Lydia would
> elope with me as Ensign Beverley, yet am I by no means certain that
> she would take me with the impediment of our friends' consent, a
> regular humdrum wedding, and the reversion of a good fortune on
> my side: no, no; I must prepare her gradually for the discovery,
> and make myself necessary to her, before I risk it ....[8]

Lydia has become so accustomed to thinking in romantic terms that
she is no longer aware of the affectation which is so evident to the
Captain. Nor does she realize that he is purposely playing up to
her. The audience knows that Lydia can not long be happy without
a fortune, but Lydia derives much pleasure and satisfaction simply
from the thought of living in poverty on love. When her lover
reveals his real identity to her, instead of rewarding him for all the
trouble she has occasioned him, Lydia makes this comment: "So!—
there will be no elopement after all!"[9] All his impetuous entreaties
bring forth only regrets on her part:

> So, while I fondly imagined we were deceiving my relations, and
> flattered myself that I should outwit and incense them all—behold
> my hopes are to be crushed at once, by my aunt's consent and appro-
> bation—and I am myself the only dupe at last! ...[10]

And she finishes her scene by deserting him, at least temporarily.

By far the most amusing scene of all is that in which Lydia

---

[7] I, 2.
[8] II, 1.
[9] IV, 2.
[10] IV, 2.

confides the details of her plight to Julia. After describing her
planned sentimental elopement—complete even to the disguise, rope
ladder, and Scotch parson—and her detestation of the conventional
marriage, Lydia recalls the thrilling escapades in which she and
her lover used to participate:

> ...How often have I stole forth, in the coldest night in January, and
> found him in the garden, stuck like a dripping statue! There would
> he kneel to me in the snow, and sneeze and cough so pathetically! he
> shivering with cold and I with apprehension! and while the freezing
> blast numbed our joints, how warmly would he press me to pity his
> flame, and glow with mutual ardour!—Ah, Julia, that was something
> like being in love.[11]

The sentimentality exhibited by Lydia Languish is in keeping
with the general taste for the romantic both in character and situation; and in Lydia, then, is to be found Sheridan's criticism of that
harmless but ridiculous phase of sentimentality consisting in an
excessive reveling in the romantic.

Julia, in the same play, represents the second phase of sentimentality noticed above, a variation consisting of an exaggerated
promenading of one's virtues. Permitting the characters to orate
on their own moral excellence and involving them in situations
which could only arouse pity on the part of the audience were essential features in the paraphernalia of eighteenth-century playwrights;
and since such characters and situations are so obviously contrary
to actual experience, the satire implied is amply warranted. Sympathy, if anything, is the emotion intended to be aroused by Julia's
Griselda-like patience and satisfaction with her betrothed. Actually, however, is there anything admirable in her passivity and in her
tiresome repetition of noble sentiments? In Sheridan's hands, the
sentimental heroine, for all her seriousness of mien, and no doubt
because of it, is a subject for caricature, and no one can fail to detect the humor in Sheridan's mock-serious treatment of her.

The undisguised exposition in the first act acquaints us with
the fact that Julia has been "contracted" to Faulkland since some
time before her father's death. So far as the audience can make
out, Faulkland's only claim to merit lies in his having rescued Julia
from drowning, but, justly opines Lydia, "I should never think of

---

[11] V, 1.

giving my heart to a man because he could swim."[12] Feeling herself thus obligated, Julia finds it necessary to defend Faulkland and make light of his weaknesses, which by far outnumber his strong points. It is, indeed, a strange sort of love which Julia bears for Faulkland, one which depends for sustenance on just such a strong sense of duty as she possesses.

Had he made the other characters in the play of a piece with Julia, Sheridan might have been warmly embraced by the advocates of the true "genteel" comedy, but his disinclination to be in their ranks is shown by his presenting Julia as the sole specimen of her kind in a play possessing a different manner, subject matter, and tempo. This contrast, more than anything else, gives the clue to Sheridan's motive in creating such a character as opposed to others who act and speak more naturally.

As an example of the type of speech considered "genteel" by Sheridan's contemporaries, Julia's words to Faulkland, on one of the numerous occasions when he is testing her love for him, are excellent:

> My soul is oppressed with sorrow at the nature of your misfortune: had these adverse circumstances arisen from a less fatal cause, I should have felt strong comfort in the thought that I could now chase from your bosom every doubt of the warm sincerity of my love. My heart has long known no other guardian—I now entrust my person to your honor—we will fly together. When safe from pursuit, my father's will may be fulfilled—and I receive a legal claim to be the partner of your sorrows, and tenderest comforter. Then on the bosom of your wedded Julia, you may lull your keen regret to slumbering; while virtuous love, with a cherub's hand, shall smooth the brow of upbraiding thought, and pluck the thorn from compunction.[13]

Obviously Julia could not have spoken as she did if she did not derive certain pleasure from considering herself an essentially moral person. Julia's case presents another instance of morality and self-approval merging into a more or less unconscious egotism. Julia's actions are of course beyond reproach, but the element of smugness is always quietly apparent. Such a speech as the one quoted above may have called forth sympathetic tears from an audience which, because of the change in moral outlook, was taking even its comedy

[12] I, 2.
[13] V, 1.

seriously; but, appearing amid the amusing notions of Lydia Languish and the "ingeniously misapplied" verbiage of Mrs. Malaprop,
it should produce the opposite effect. Julia's condoning of Faulkland's capriciousness is unforgivable, because it is all too evident
that he will never be able to resist this perpetual prying into her
soul. Julia herself laments: "O woman! how true should be your
judgment, when your resolution is so weak!"[14] Lack of resolution
was, unfortunately, characteristic of the heroines of the comedy of
sensibility.

Had Sheridan created for Maria a role calling for more than
four entrances which almost at once resolve into as many exits,
he would have given the audience another Julia. Maria is obviously included as additional satire on the genteel-comedy heroine
of the day when it was customary for writers to exhibit the virtues
of society rather than its vices. Like Julia, Maria possesses a high
sense of duty and loyalty as well as the usual docility and seriousness of purpose. Like all the sentimental ladies, she conveys the
impression of having been mistreated. Her virtues are even more
apparent in contrast to the follies of the heterogeneous company in
which she finds herself. It is not that Maria is unnecessarily decorous or irreproachable; it is merely that her general make-up is
too sensible and restricted for a world where nonsense and care-
free actions are in order. Amongst characters whose idiosyncrasies
might well have given them a place in a Jonsonian comedy, Maria's
sober virtue is noticeably out of place. In love with the profligate
Charles, she is deterred by her sense of rectitude from making an
outright admission of the fact, and, accordingly, she consigns her
love to a status of pity until a more propitious time shall arrive.
When Charles is exonerated of his misdemeanors, the only obstacle
preventing Maria's declaration is the rumor linking him with Lady
Sneerwell. As soon as this rumor is disposed of, the way is clear
for the usual happy close, in which virtue is as usual triumphant,
but unexciting, to say the least.

The Walter to Julia's Griselda is the role played by the mis-
guided Faulkland to whom Julia has given heart and hand. In
regard to Faulkland, the sentimentality finds expression in a kind
of self-torture which, though obviously of serious consequence to

---

[14] V, 3.

himself and the suffering Julia, is ludicrous and contemptible in the eyes of others. He has set up an impossible lovers' code, with every detail of which he expects Julia to comply. According to Faulkland, true lovers should never be gay, in fact, *can* never be gay, when away from each other. The mere report of his lady's well-being in his absence vexes him so that he exclaims:

> Hell and the devil! There!—there—I told you so! I told you so! Oh! she thrives in my absence!—Dancing! but her whole feelings have been in opposition with mine;—I have been anxious, silent, pensive, sedentary—my days have been hours of care, my nights of watchfulness.—She has been all health! spirit! song! dance!—Oh! damned, damned levity![15]

This is typical of the way Faulkland carries on when he is away from Julia. When he is with her, however, his over-possessiveness becomes even more obnoxious, for then his "captious, unsatisfied temper" makes him indulge in a perpetual questioning and fathoming of her love, which makes Julia miserable and nearly drives Faulkland to distraction. Yet he will not desist until Julia finally threatens to terminate matters entirely by rejecting her lover, although at the close of the play all is of course forgiven. Like Walter in the old story, Faulkland never ceases to be surprised at each new revelation of her virtue, and is always eager to investigate her patience further. Even such a procedure might be justifiable, were the results allowed to remain final. Faulkland, however, will not consider relinquishing his claims on Julia and seeking another who may, perchance, measure up to his requirements, and for this reason his actions can not possibly be condoned. The fact that Julia not only equals but exceeds these expectations, and that Faulkland, blinded by his own conceit, does not recognize her excellence is what makes him all the more ridiculous a figure. In the same way Julia's repeated acceptance of his ill-treatment exposes her to well-deserved criticism. To make matters worse, Faulkland seems to derive peculiar delight from lamenting upon the various unfortunate aspects of his love affair. He explains to Julia his theory of behavior for lovers as follows:

---

[15] II, 1.

.. For such is my temper, Julia, that I should regard every mirth-
ful moment in your absence as a treason to constancy. The mutual
tear that steals down the cheek of parting lovers is a compact, that
no smile shall live there till they meet again.[16]

The foregoing, then, is love on the genteel plan which permitted words to speak louder than actions, and catered to false
delicacy rather than to sincerity. The drama of sensibility was not
an imitation of contemporary life, but a completely artificial set-up,
which in turn invited imitation by its observers. True sentiment had
given way to sentimentality, and even Sheridan and Goldsmith were
not influential enough to restore the comic drama to normality.

Not content with a general satire on the sentimentality preva-
lent in the contemporary theatre, Sheridan selected the most conspicuous aspect of it—hypocrisy—for further attention. Both audience and playwrights were gradually becoming aware that sentimentality carried to excess was in itself a literary sin. Nothing,
however, deserved ridicule so much as this same sentimentality
when hypocrisy was its distinguishing feature. Sheridan concen-
trated upon this particular social fault in the character of his arch-
hypocrite, Joseph Surface.

The practice of hypocrisy is such an exceedingly common one
that it is almost continually under the scourge of the satirist, who
thrives for the most part on unmasking deceit. The subtler the
art of the perpetrator of this folly is, the sweeter is the revenge of
the discoverer; and since the hypocrisy of Joseph Surface was so
nearly second nature with him, the enjoyment Sheridan must have
derived from presenting and exposing it is easily imagined.

As usual, Sheridan's dramatic technique calls for discussion of
a character by those already assembled on the stage before the actual
introduction of the character in question. Thus, early in the first
act there takes place the following confidential interlude between
Lady Sneerwell, the leader of the gossiping school, and Snake, one
of her tools:

Lady Sneer. ...I know him to be artful, selfish, and malicious—
in short, a sentimental knave; while with Sir Peter, and indeed with
all his acquaintance, he, passes for a youthful miracle of prudence,
good sense, and benevolence.

---

[16] III, 2.

> *Snake.* Yes; yet Sir Peter vows he has not his equal in England; and, above all, he praises him as a man of sentiment.
>
> *Lady Sneer.* True; and with the assistance of his sentiment and hyprocrisy he has brought Sir Peter entirely into his interest with regard to Maria; while poor Charles has no friend in the house—though, I fear, he has a powerful one in Maria's heart, against whom we must direct our schemes.[17]

In this way Sheridan invariably informs the audience of the proper attitude to hold in regard to the characters introduced. There is no attempt, therefore, to conceal the true nature of Joseph Surface, who is himself so proficient in the art of dissembling that very few of his acquaintances ever suspect it. He is obliged to minimize his duplicity when in the company of Lady Sneerwell since they know each other too well. It is this common knowledge that forces them into a compact to further each other's interests. Surface is ever watching the main chance, yet he obviously takes pleasure in conveying an impression of thoughtfulness and generosity through his feigned consideration for others. By this means he manages to insinuate himself into that good repute which belongs rightfully to his brother Charles. The following bit of conversation with Lady Sneerwell illustrates the type of sentiment in which Joseph Surface indulges regularly and reveals the poseur he really is:

> *Jos. Surf.* True, madam; notwithstanding his vices, one can't help feeling for him. Poor Charles! I'm sure I wish it were in my power to be of any essential service to him; for the man who does not share in the distresses of a brother, even though merited by his own misconduct, deserves—
>
> *Lady Sneer.* O Lud! you are going to be moral, and forget that you are among friends.
>
> *Jos. Surf.* Egad, that's true! I'll keep that sentiment till I see Sir Peter....[18]

This is a mild example of Joseph's customary solicitude. Generally he is more insufferable with his veneer of sympathies and considerations.

There is another rather unexpected aspect to this type of drama, for the more noble, morally, the character considers himself, the more satisfied with himself is he likely to become. In this way

---

[17] *The School for Scandal,* I, 1.
[18] I, 1.

egotism links itself up with moralizing, since the individual indulges in it because he approves of himself as being a moral person. In the authentic genteel comedy, sentimentalizing and moralizing were part of the ordinary course of things, and the humor of the situation was always to be found in the ultra-seriousness of the thought and speech. In regard to Mr. Surface the satire is rendered greater in proportion to his own duplicity.

Whether or not Sheridan was indebted for his Joseph Surface to Congreve's characterization of Maskwell can not be determined, but there is sufficient similarity between the two double-dealers to warrant such an assumption, particularly since the Congrevean influence on Sheridan is a self-evident fact. But Maskwell did not depend upon moral circumlocutions and lofty sentiments to aid him in carrying out his plans; in this respect Joseph Surface deviates from the earlier model.

Having acquainted the audience with Joseph's character, Sheridan wastes no time in developing the satire. Every moral speech assigned to this character, therefore, is a single pencil-stroke of criticism, as it were, in the outline to be completed at the close of the play. Even when in the company of his back-biting friends, Joseph can not throw off the cloak of genteel respectability which he has found so convenient to don on every other occasion, although his insincerity is so evident that his utterances always reflect the contrary intent of his mind. His winning card is the suave manner in which he poses as the exponent of the attributes of brotherly love. How seriously concerned he appears when his friends are discussing Charles's affairs: "This may be entertainment to you, gentlemen, but you pay very little regard to the feelings of a brother."[19] Maria, intolerant of similar exhibitions of malice by the company, is forced to leave them. Joseph imposes upon Maria, likewise, when he offers the following gem in answer to her comment that malicious gossip is the result of bitterness of mind:

> Undoubtedly, madam; and it has always been a sentiment of mine, that to propagate a malicious truth wantonly is more despicable than to falsify from revenge....[20]

---

[19] I, 2.
[20] II, 3.

Sir Peter Teazle, one of Joseph's unsuspecting admirers, is given to flattering his young friend, and it is to be regretted that his loyalty to Joseph is misplaced.

> *Sir Pet.* Oh, my dear friend, the goodness of your own heart misleads you. You judge of others by yourself.
> *Jos. Surf.* Certainly, Sir Peter, the heart that is conscious of its own integrity is ever slow to credit another's treachery.[21]

This occurs when Sir Peter intimates that Charles Surface is breaking up his happy wedded life, but Joseph, playing the man of sentiment and an affectionate brother, has a defense all ready:

> Oh, 'tis not to be credited! There may be a man capable of such baseness, to be sure; but, for my part, till you can give me positive proofs, I cannot but doubt it. However, if it should be proved on him, he is no longer a brother of mine—I disclaim kindred with him: for the man who can break the laws of hospitality, and tempt the wife of his friend, deserves to be branded as the pest of society.[22]

That Joseph's sentiments are precisely the opposite of those indicated in this heroic speech is of course obvious to everyone but Sir Peter, who believes "there is nothing in the world so noble as a man of sentiment!"[23] That Sheridan's view is precisely the opposite of Sir Peter's is likewise intentionally obvious to all, particularly since Sheridan expresses it through a character not meant to be taken seriously by the audience. A little later in the same scene Sheridan permits Charles to supplement the meaning, if not the words, of Sir Peter's statement, giving it the proper interpretation. It is the famous discovery scene of the play when Sir Peter is confronted by the spectacle of his wife in Joseph's room. Joseph, for once, dares to say nothing, and this affords Charles the opportunity for reiteration:

> ...Brother, I'm sorry to find you have given that worthy man grounds for so much uneasiness.—Sir Peter! there's nothing in the world so noble as a man of sentiment! (*Exit.*)[24]

---

[21] IV, 3.
[22] IV, 3.
[23] IV, 3.
[24] IV, 3.

Old Rowley, the friend of both Sir Peter and Sir Oliver Surface, accurately characterizes Joseph. In answer to Sir Oliver's conviction that Joseph "has a string of charitable sentiments at his fingers' ends," Rowley comments: "Or, rather, at his tongue's end, Sir Oliver; for I believe there is no sentiment he has such faith in as that *Charity begins at home.*"[25]

These five characters, then,—Lydia Languish, Julia, Maria, Faulkland, and Joseph Surface—afforded ample opportunity for Sheridan to develop his satire on the various phases of sentimentality. Although he expended his greatest efforts in this endeavor in *The Rivals,* which he deliberately utilized for this purpose, he introduced satirical bits throughout his dramatic composition.

That notable farce *The Critic,* for example, served more than one purpose. It brought up to date the outmoded line of critical pieces which included such successes as Beaumont and Fletcher's *The Knight of the Burning Pestle,* a satire on the currently popular plays based upon medieval romances; Buckingham's *The Rehearsal,* a burlesque directed at the heroic drama then holding sway; Gay's *The Beggar's Opera,* a farce satirizing contemporary politics and the trend of English opera in imitation of the Italian; and finally Fielding's *Tom Thumb,* a burlesque attacking the stereotyped contemporary tragedies. *The Critic* surpassed all these in its frank criticism of the current fashion in drama. The mock-serious lashing it administered to sentimental literature was one of the most effective single triumphs so far achieved among the various attempts to ameliorate the situation into which the drama, in particular, and all literature, in general, had fallen. The prologue itself is one of the most significant features of the play, and illustrates Sheridan's views on genteel comedy. It is here that his impatience with the affectations of the drama of sensibility is most conspicuous. Regarding the transformation that comedy had undergone since the Restoration, Sheridan opines:

> . . .,
> The reformation to extremes has run.
> The frantic hero's wild delirium past,
> Now insipidity succeeds bombast; . . .

---

[25] V, 1.

Sheridan did not maintain this attitude consistently, however. His desire for popularity often turned him aside, temporarily, from the main course, and for this reason he did not accomplish as much as he might otherwise have done in chasing the "arrant prude," genteel comedy, from the stage.

The lack of humor in the genteel comedy had become so complete that the line of demarcation between this tearful comedy and the ordinary tragedy was now barely perceptible. The real situation, as Sheridan saw it, is summed up in the words between Critic Dangle's level-headed wife and the upstart play agent, Sneer, who has brought a play for Dangle to read. The seriousness of the play forces Dangle to ask if it is a tragedy, and the conversation continues:

> *Sneer.* No, that's a genteel comedy, not a translation—only taken from the French: it is written in a style which they have lately tried to run down; the true sentimental, and nothing ridiculous in it from the beginning to the end.
>
> *Mrs. Dang.* Well, if they had kept to that, I should not have been such an enemy to the stage; there was some edification to be got from those pieces, Mr. Sneer!
>
> *Sneer.* I am quite of your opinion, Mrs. Dangle: the theatre, in proper hands, might certainly be made the school of morality; but now, I am sorry to say it, people seem to go there principally for their entertainment!
>
> *Mrs. Dang.* It would have been more to the credit of the managers to have kept it in the other line.[26]

Sheridan thus emphasizes the ridiculous aspect of genteel comedy, which by its make-shift morality could never be accepted as a desirable substitute for true comedy.

As for women, Sheridan did not have Congreve's idealistic conception of woman as a superior creature for whom must be reserved the most beautiful and most eloquent passages. For Sheridan there could be no such partiality. In his plays charming men appear as frequently as do charming women; and the less admirable characters are equally distributed between the sexes. After reading Congreve, one remembers the scintillating Millamant and her train, which boasts of such ladies as Belinda, Cynthia, and Angelica. Not so consistent was Sheridan in the types of women he pre-

---

[26] *The Critic,* I, 1.

sented, and the heroines who linger longest in the mind vary from the ultra-romantic Lydia Languish and the patient Julia to the faithful Maria and the transplanted country hoyden, Lady Teazle. Like Congreve, Sheridan had a first-hand knowledge of women, but he chose to make other use of it. Instead of selecting women whose admirable qualities would attract attention by their rarity and beauty, he preferred more ordinary portraits which would prove attractive in spite of certain less commendable attributes. Indeed, Sheridan seems to have chosen his outstanding female characters more for their idiosyncrasies than for any intrinsically poetic values they might possess.

Female pretensions to education are satirized in Mrs. Malaprop. In commenting upon *The Rivals*, Nicoll expresses the opinion that "the continuous stream of infelicitous verbiage which flows from the mouth of Mrs. Malaprop begins after a time to pall..."[27] The criticism is a just one when the play is considered simply as closet drama, for then one peruses the material in a leisurely fashion and does not overlook a single malapropism. In that light the lady's chatter may become tedious indeed, since eventually the novelty of her misused words must wear off. Considering the play as a living thing on the stage, however, one can no longer accept outright Nicoll's statement, for the rapidity of Sheridan's style never permits any one scene to lag long enough to become boring. The good-natured humor underlying each situation occupies the audience so completely that such matters as the frequency or monotony of Mrs. Malaprop's utterances are lightly passed over. Although the contrivance Sheridan employs in presenting Mrs. Malaprop's "select words so ingeniously misapplied, without being mispronounced"[28] becomes obviously mechanical at times, it does not deserve much criticism on this score. It is merely another instance of Sheridan's insight into the commonplace methods of procuring laughter from the audience. The more sensitive the auditor is to shades of meaning in his vocabulary, the more readily does he respond to each cue offered by Mrs. Malaprop. The resulting laughter is not the intellectual mirth inspired by high comedy; it is closer in spirit to the ready laugh at each turn and tumble of the

---

[27] *XVIII Century Drama, 1750-1800*, p. 160.
[28] *The Rivals*, I, 2.

clown, but is elevated by the use of verbal rather than physical acrobatics.

Mrs. Malaprop exhibits two outstanding foibles: one of these consists in her pretensions to youth; the other, to education. There is nothing in her make-up to suggest the "superannuated frippery" of Congreve's Lady Wishfort, but there are several characteristics shared by the two. Both are conceited women who fancy that theirs has been a superior education, although in reality neither one has much to offer along that line. As *femmes savantes* they rate ridiculously low, but they achieve distinction of a different type by means of their unusual vocabularies. Beside the disreputable language of Lady Wishfort, that of Mrs. Malaprop has an air of refinement. The words are at least respectable, although, by appearing at the wrong times, they give another impression. Like Lady Wishfort, Mrs. Malaprop also has confidence in her ability to attract men, and is likewise disillusioned in her attempted love affair. Like Lady Wishfort, Mrs. Malaprop too has a niece whose life she tries to regulate. The latter guardian, however, is a much more likeable person, and the satire directed against her is never bitter as is that against Lady Wishfort. Occasionally she brings to mind Colman and Garrick's Mrs. Heidelberg,[29] another influential aunt who has become famous through her amusing verbal manipulations. But Mrs. Heidelberg's claim to fame rests not upon her misuse of words but upon her mispronunciation of them.

Sheridan was not merely satirizing the follies represented in Mrs. Malaprop; he was utilizing her as a laugh-provoker as well. He was not the cynic Congreve was. Sheridan found much to criticize in contemporary society, but whether or not his criticisms were taken seriously by this society was not to him a matter of vital concern. Above all he liked to please, and if he pleased by the humor of a situation rather than by the satire therein, he was satisfied. In creating the character of Mrs. Malaprop, Sheridan was satirizing all those old women who have a mistaken idea of their own importance and who enjoy upsetting the course of true love. To complete the caricature, Sheridan has her make use of all the verbal blunders he can invent. The inappropriateness of her words contrasts strik-

---

[29] Colman, George, Sr., and Garrick, David, *The Clandestine Marriage,* 1766.

ingly with her seriousness of mien, and this misuse of words distorts ludicrously each statement she proffers, placing her entirely at the mercy of the audience and the other characters in the play.

Mrs. Malaprop's views on education and marriage are almost too well known to bear repetition, but certain passages are indispensable to any discussion of the "old weather-beaten she-dragon,"[30] as Captain Absolute calls her in a letter to his Lydia. The most amusing of her effusions is instigated by a harmless query from Sir Anthony.

> *Sir Anth.* Why, Mrs. Malaprop, in moderation now, what would you have a woman know?
> *Mrs. Mal.* Observe me, Sir Anthony. I would by no means wish a daughter of mine to be a progeny of learning; I don't think so much learning becomes a young woman; for instance, I would never let her meddle with Greek, or Hebrew, or algebra, or simony, or fluxions, or paradoxes, or such inflammatory branches of learning—neither would it be necessary for her to handle any of your mathematical, astronomical, diabolical instruments.—But, Sir Anthony, I would send her, at nine years old, to a boarding-school, in order to learn a little ingenuity and artifice. Then, as she grew up, I would have her instructed in geometry, that she might know something of the contagious countries;—but, above all, Sir Anthony, she should be mistress of orthodoxy, that she might not misspell, and mispronounce words so shamefully as girls usually do; and likewise that she might reprehend the true meaning of what she is saying. This, Sir Anthony, is what I would have a woman know;—and I don't think there is a superstitious article in it.[31]

This single quotation serves as an index to her character. The self-assurance and dignity evident in the speech are truly admirable, but her innocent substitutions of the wrong words in the right places destroy any common sense originally intended. There is not so much of the intellect-quickening wit of Congreve to be found in Sheridan's characterization. Sheridan did not always strive for the clear, cold wit of high comedy, of Congreve or of Molière; he enjoyed the rich, generous laughter awakened by direct humor, whether of character or situation. The profusion of humorless sentimentality had so weakened eighteenth-century comedy that the metallic tinkle produced by the clash of wits in the Congrevean com-

---

[30] *The Rivals*, III, 3.
[31] I, 2.

edy was entirely lacking. Mrs. Malaprop, however, is an indication of the return to true comedy as illustrated in the plays of Goldsmith and Sheridan.

An excellent satirical scene is that which takes place between
Mrs. Malaprop and Captain Absolute when the latter, at his father's
instigation, has come to ask for the hand of Lydia Languish. No
one is aware that Ensign Beverley, who has already won Lydia's
heart, is the Captain disguised as his own rival. This mistake in
identity made by Lydia's aunt leaves the way open for numerous
sallies which are appreciated only by the Captain and the audience.

Mrs. Malaprop is easily influenced by flattery, and a few well-
chosen phrases, particularly phrases complimenting her intellectual
achievements, are sufficient to bring her over to the Captain's side.
Her modest rejoinder to his praises is that "few gentlemen, now-a-
days, know how to value the ineffectual qualities in women! few
think how a little knowledge becomes a gentlewoman!"[32] Having
decided to take him into her confidence, she even allows him to read
a letter from Beverley which she "interceded." It appears that in
this letter Captain Absolute, *alias* Beverley, has made certain derog-
atory remarks about Mrs. Malaprop's manner of speaking. According to her own opinion, these remarks are most unjust, for,
"if I reprehend any thing in this world, it is the use of my oracular
tongue, and a nice derangement of epitaphs!"[33] Unwittingly, Mrs.
Malaprop becomes the go-between in an interview between her niece
and the Captain, little dreaming that this is the very man she wants
Lydia to avoid. Even though Lydia persists in calling him "Beverley," she arouses not her aunt's suspicions but her apologies. Mrs.
Malaprop is amazed at Lydia's apparent impudence and explains
that "there's nothing to be hoped for from her! she's as headstrong
as an allegory on the banks of Nile."[34]

In the next act is the recognition scene wherein Mrs. Malaprop,
Lydia, and Sir Anthony Absolute discover the extent of Captain
Absolute's dissembling. Mrs. Malaprop's chagrin is most evident
when she perceives that young Absolute has finally made a dupe of
her; but, realizing that any further protestation upon her part will

---

[32] III, 3.
[33] III, 3.
[34] III, 3.

be of no avail, she is willing to take Sir Anthony's advice and forgive and forget the escapade.

> *Mrs. Mal.* Well, Sir Anthony, since you desire it, we will not
> anticipate the past!—so mind, young people—our restrospection will
> be all to the future.[35]

Thus a generous side of her nature is revealed in contrast with her
customary vanity and affected superiority.

Sheridan concludes the satire by involving Mrs. Malaprop in
a one-sided love affair with Sir Lucius O'Trigger, a stupid, conceited Hibernian, who fancies he has been corresponding with a
seventeen-year old girl. Eventually there is the "show-down," and
poor Mrs. Malaprop is forced to admit that it is she who has been
the author of the romantic letters. To Sir Lucius the revelation is
of little consequence, but to the woman spurned the unwelcome
reception of her romantic intentions is indeed humiliating. It is
an expected finishing touch to the portrait of the vain old woman
who has ambitions for herself as well as for her niece, and whose
ambitions lead her into such amusing predicaments.

Although there is nothing novel in the appearance of this stock
character who is invariably the butt of ridicule in comedy and tragedy alike, this guardian is a rather pleasant variation. Beneath the
general satire there is to be found constantly Sheridan's good-
natured humor. The audience is not asked to look upon and despise
Mrs. Malaprop for her idiosyncrasies; it is, on the contrary, invited
to witness and laugh at her follies. Sheridan was fond of exposing
the weaknesses of his characters, but he never designed to rout
these foibles; he aimed to please, and found the art of satire most
suited to his métier. In only one respect does Sheridan fall short
of the prescribed formula for eighteenth-century comedies: there
is no happy ending in store for Mrs. Malaprop; there are only the
good wishes of Sir Anthony, who orders all to "drink a health to
the young couples, and a husband to Mrs. Malaprop."[36] Having
played a prominent part in the affairs of her niece, and having set
herself up as an authority on language and love, she is now relegated
to a position of minor importance; and there is no indication that
she will profit by her experience.

---

[35] IV, 2.

[36] V, 3.

In *The School for Scandal* Sheridan continues his practice of depicting various phases of eighteenth-century society. This play is one of the finest examples there are of the comedy of manners, and as such, it presents a highly realistic picture of the artificial society of that day. Here once again the spirit is that of Molière and Congreve, of *Le Misanthrope* and *The Way of the World.* The plot of the play is Congrevean in its complication; but the characters, like Congreve's Millamant and Mirabell, show unquestionably the influence of the sophisticated creations of Molière.

There is perhaps more sarcasm in this play than anywhere else in Sheridan, for he was sincere in his criticism of malicious gossip. Being a man of the mode, he was constantly coming into contact with the idlers of high society who had nothing better to do than to destroy good reputations and substitute bad ones. Genial as he was, he could not take part in the practice of scandal-mongering; instead, he wrote *The School for Scandal,* a satire upon this disreputable sport of the beaus and belles.

Although Lady Sneerwell is obviously the motivating force in the "school for scandal," she is not so adept in the art as Mrs. Candour. The latter best illustrates the type of person who indulges in scandal-mongering for her own amusement. There is no subtlety in her procedure; she merely retails each idle rumor she has heard in her travels about the town and pounces on anything that remotely suggests a scandal. An important feature in Mrs. Candour's reportorial technique is the method of insinuation which contrasts ironically with her affected innocence of intention. The implication of each piece of gossip she relates is exactly the opposite of its accompanying apologetic remark. The best example of Mrs. Candour's ordinary conversation comes in answer to the moral Maria's opinion that the reporters of gossip are as guilty as those who invent it.

> *Mrs. Can.* To be sure they are; tale-bearers are as bad as the tale-makers—'tis an old observation, and a very true one: but what's to be done, as I said before? how will you prevent people from talking? To-day, Mrs. Clackitt assured me, Mr. and Mrs. Honeymoon were at last become mere man and wife, like the rest of their acquaintance....And at the same time Miss Tattle, who was by, affirmed, that Lord Buffalo had discovered his lady at a house of no extraordinary fame; and that Sir Harry Bouquet and Tom Saunter were to measure swords on a similar provocation. But, Lord, do you think

I would report these things! No, no! tale-bearers, as I said before, are just as bad as the tale-makers.[37]

And the hypocritical Joseph Surface, wishing to make a good impression in Maria's company, comments appropriately: "Ah! Mrs. Candour, if every body had your forbearance and good nature!"

Lady Sneerwell, on the other hand, is not so amiable a character. She represents the type who gossip for the sole purpose of defaming others, regardless of whether or not the victims deserve such ill-treatment. With her the motive is revenge, as she explains to Snake, one of her tools. "Wounded myself, in the early part of my life, by the envenomed tongue of slander, I confess I have since known no pleasure equal to the reducing others to the level of my own reputation."[38] With this selfish motive constantly in mind, Lady Sneerwell becomes, in a sense, the protagonist of the play, for the complications in the several love affairs arise from her machinations. She attempts to break up the romance between Charles Surface and Maria because she herself is interested in Charles. For this purpose she utilizes Joseph Surface as an ally, since Joseph in turn is interested in Maria and has already alienated her guardian's (Sir Peter's) affections from Charles. Her plans come to naught, however, for Sir Peter discovers Joseph's duplicity when he stumbles, accidentally, upon what appears to be a liaison between Joseph and Lady Teazle. Finally there is the testimony of Snake, who admits that Lady Sneerwell originated and circulated rumors concerning an affair between herself and Charles, and that she even went so far as to forge letters in Charles's hand confirming his love for her. Joseph's defense of her is a surprisingly weak one, and, foiled in her attempts to acquire love and revenge, Lady Sneerwell is obliged to withdraw from the scene, humiliated and disappointed.

As a third example in this category of female gossips may be included Lady Teazle, the country girl whom Sir Peter married and took back with him to London. She joins the "scandalous college" because it is apparently the fashion of fine society to gossip and she wishes to acquire the mark of sophistication which membership in that society seems to imply. She becomes so proficient in the tech-

---

[37] *The School for Scandal,* I, 1.
[38] I, 1.

nique of destroying reputations that Lady Sneerwell herself offers faint praise in the comment: "Very well, Lady Teazle; I see you can be a little severe."[39] Lady Teazle has no intention of being malicious, however; she indulges in gossip for the same reason that she purchases a new gown—that of maintaining her position as a woman of fashion. When she attempts to defend her acquaintances as "people of rank and fortune, and remarkably tenacious of reputation," Sir Peter tallies: "Yes, egad, they are tenacious of reputation with a vengeance; for they don't choose anybody should have a character but themselves!"[40] Whereas Sir Peter considers gossip a matter of serious concern, his wife looks upon it as mere amusement. It is not until she experiences for herself the effects of this seemingly innocuous entertainment that she realizes how harmful gossip can be. When her own happiness comes perilously near to being destroyed as a result of the rumors circulated by Lady Sneerwell and her circle, Lady Teazle resolves to forego the pleasure of their company.

These women represent three types of tale-bearers frequently encountered in every class of society. They are not the only figures used by Sheridan in satirizing the general subject of gossip; in the background are others, like Mrs. Clackitt, who appear incidentally in the conversation. No discussion of gossip, however, is complete without consideration of the part played by men therein, particularly in the comedy of manners, which encourages the exchange of idle rumors and the talk of the town.

To assist the "daughters of calumny" in culling and distributing the current bits of slander, Sheridan has provided four males: Joseph Surface, Snake, Sir Benjamin Backbite, and his uncle Crabtree.

The first one may be summarily dismissed. A hypocrite by nature, he can not even be consistent in his attitude to the malicious members of his society. He represents the male counterpart of Lady Sneerwell, for both take part in this slanderous reciprocity primarily for selfish reasons rather than for any light amusement they may derive. He is not a true gossip like Mrs. Candour, whose manner of tale-bearing is so diverting to her observers; he merely

---

[39] II, 2.
[40] II, 2.

contributes to the school by participating in and furthering Lady Sneerwell's projects when there is a chance for individual gain on his part.

Snake is a caricature of the social sycophant. Everything about him suggests exaggeration, even his opinion of himself. His duties as a club-member are menial ones, such as carrying out Lady Sneerwell's orders, forging letters, starting rumors on their way, or perhaps inserting certain paragraphs in the papers. Even Joseph Surface's admonitions do not arouse her suspicions about Snake; and because she believes Snake to be sincere, she entrusts him with her most secret plans. It is not until the close of the play, when Snake sells his services to a higher bidder, that Lady Sneerwell realizes the extent of his perfidy. In making the way clear for the usual satisfactory ending, Joseph Surface turns moral again and, in order to appear in a more favorable light, finds it necessary to betray Lady Sneerwell. To do so, he bribes Snake to tell the truth about his employer's schemes to wreck the happiness of the Surfaces and the Teazles. Before Snake leaves, however, he begs the company to keep secret the fact that he has divulged the required information about Lady Sneerwell. When Sir Peter accuses him of being "ashamed of having done a right thing once in your life," Snake replies: "Ah, sir, consider—I live by the badness of my character; and, if it were once known that I had been betrayed into an honest action, I should lose every friend I have in the world."[41] And in that observation is revealed the true nature of Snake, the flattering, insincere parasite, who prides himself on his disreputable calling.

The real rivals of Mrs. Candour are two other notable male slanderers, Sir Benjamin Backbite and his uncle Crabtree. They are very much alike, except for the fact that Sir Benjamin poses as a wit and a poet, whereas both men bear greater resemblance to the "wittols" of Congreve than to the true wits. They work as a team, one generally acting as the chorus while the other takes charge of the narration. Crabtree acts as publicity-manager for his nephew, acquainting all who will listen with reports of Sir Benjamin's talents. Lady Sneerwell and her friends are aware of Sir Benjamin's artistic limitations, but he and his uncle are necessary to the society because of the numerous items of gossip they always contribute to

---

[41] V, 3.

the conversation. Not only does Sir Benjamin have pretensions to education and wit, but he has aspirations to the hand of Maria, who can not even tolerate him. Indeed, he has written love elegies for Maria, which, Crabtree insists, will immortalize the young lady. At his uncle's prodding, and after the proper amount of hesitation, Sir Benjamin gives examples of his wit as it appears in charades, ordinary conversation, and epigrams which he can turn out while on horseback, so ingenious is he. He and his uncle know all the news of the town, and their inventive powers function so readily that they are able to manufacture all the details they are unable to ascertain.

Their taste for the sensational turns the vague account of Sir Peter's discovery of his wife in Joseph Surface's apartment into a detailed report including a duel between the two men in which Sir Peter is dangerously wounded. The best opportunity for viewing the "school for scandal" in action appears when they arrive *en masse* at Sir Peter's house for discussion of the particulars. Mrs. Candour is the first to come to the meeting, but the others soon follow. Almost immediately there ensues a heated debate regarding the various and conflicting accounts. Sir Benjamin and Crabtree alarm Lady Sneerwell considerably when they insist that Charles, and not Joseph, was the man involved with Sir Peter in the duel. The news of the duel upsets Mrs. Candour, also, for she had not yet been informed of this aspect of the situation. The four gossips then proceed to reconstruct the story. There emerges a detailed, though somewhat confusing, account of the circumstances leading to the duel, which Crabtree affirms was fought with pistols rather than swords as his nephew maintains. Crabtree concludes as follows:

> ...Charles's shot took effect, as I tell you, and Sir Peter's missed; but, what is very extraordinary, the ball struck against a little bronze Shakespeare that stood over the fireplace, grazed out of the window at a right angle, and wounded the postman, who was just coming to the door with a double letter from Northamptonshire.[42]

This seems to be a fairly satisfactory and colorful version, and the company is almost ready to give credence to it when Sir Oliver

---

[42] IV, 2.

Surface, the uncle of Charles and Joseph, arrives to discredit the story. Sir Peter himself soon appears and, when he can no longer tolerate their feigned efforts at consolation and their more obvious attempts at criticism, orders the scandal-mongers out of his house. All that remains now is the final scene which reveals the perfidies of Lady Sneerwell and makes the exposé of the "school for scandal" complete. Lady Teazle's denunciation of the society brings the scandalous episode of the play to a close.

There is no suggestion that this satirical portrayal of one of the most influential social cliques essays to correct its foibles. Like many others who have dealt with the follies of certain sections of society, Sheridan was aware that even the most scathing treatment of gossip could not be depended upon to terminate its Hydra-like existence, and, like them, too, he did not take the existing situation too seriously to heart. Satire is not always bent on reform, though it often is and sometimes does succeed. Sheridan doubtless would have been flattered to learn that any of his audience went home resolved never to gossip again, but the reforming instinct was incidental to his general purpose to provide entertainment. For this reason he was content when his audiences went away pleased with the evening's diversion, rather than troubled by the suggested morals.

Sheridan may have found that his ridicule of the "school for scandal" was of too brief duration for an evening's entertainment at the theatre; he may, also, have desired to follow the practice of earlier and contemporary dramatists in creating intricate plots in which to entangle the characters. Whatever his reason may have been, the complications in this play are on a par with those of almost any of the Restoration comedies of manners, with the exception, perhaps, of *The Way of the World,* a masterpiece of plot complexity. There is, in addition to the portions aimed at the gossips and scandal-mongers which give the play its title, a second plot consisting of a satirical portrait of the old bachelor who takes unto himself a young wife and is not sure he can keep her. The same plot served Wycherley for an entire play, *The Country Wife,* but for Sheridan, who used it in its expurgated form, it merely supplements the "scandal" episodes and introduces some real sentiment into the comedy. Both Sir Peter and Lady Teazle are contributions to the sentimental school of the day, and both have genuine appeal.

The only others in the play who inspire the same sort of feeling are Charles Surface and his uncle, Sir Oliver Surface, who, together with the hypocritical Joseph, are involved in a third plot. This third plot concerns the efforts of Sir Oliver to discover which of his two nephews is more deserving of his bounty. The three separate trends of the play are expertly interwoven, each having direct bearing on the other, and in the final scenes all are completely and satisfactorily merged.

As an indication of Sheridan's ability to select plots of lasting merit, one needs only to recall the numerous performances his plays have enjoyed down to the present day. Nor was he unwise in choosing Wycherley's play for adaptation. The subject under discussion is of interest to any sophisticated society, and the successful performances of *The Country Wife* in Connecticut,[43] in the summer of 1935, and in New York and London, in the 1936-37 season, are evidence of its enduring qualities.

Sheridan makes of Sir Peter Teazle a far pleasanter person than the earlier prototypes, Wycherley's Pinchwife and even Congreve's Fondlewife. Although Sir Peter finds himself in a similar predicament, also having married a girl from the country, he reacts in a more gentlemanly fashion than Pinchwife or Fondlewife. Sir Peter is a man of much common sense except in regard to his wife. Like Pinchwife, he was very circumspect in making his marital choice and selected a quiet, unpresuming young lady. He then made the same mistake of taking his wife to London. Pinchwife's jealousy was of so violent a type that it compelled him to keep his Margery under lock and key; Fondlewife thought he was being wary when he secured a parson to stay with his wife; Sir Peter, however, trusts Lady Teazle and blames himself for her indiscretions. He realizes that he ought not to expect too much from such a marriage, but he can not help wishing that he might get more out of it than the mere privilege of paying for her extravagances. The satire is directed at his vexatious disposition which, as in Faulkland's case, makes him tease his wife to ascertain whether or not she returns his love for her. Her constant evasions of his queries and the fear that their gossiping acquaintances may discover that the Teazles are not happily married make Sir Peter miserable. In a sense he is

---

[43] *News-Week*, July 13, 1935, p. 22.

proud of his wife for her ability to mix in this worldly society, but he is afraid that this same participation will make her dissatisfied with her old husband. When he finally does suspect her of imprudence in connection with one of the Surfaces, he is most angry with himself for not being able to keep her at home. He is jealous of anything or anyone that intrudes upon her time and keeps her away from him; for this reason he disapproves of her ambition to be a lady of fashion. After a while he finds that he derives certain pleasure from teasing her and thereby detaining her from her extravagant and malicious friends. It is, indeed, a somewhat negative pleasure, but Lady Teazle's repartee delights him and is reward enough for the ex-bachelor in love. After one of their little verbal combats, in which his wife generally emerges the victor, Sir Peter soliloquizes:

> So—I have gained much by my intended expostulation! Yet with what a charming air she contradicts every thing I say, and how pleasantly she shows her contempt for my authority; Well, though I can't make her love me, there is great satisfaction in quarrelling with her; and I think she never appears to such advantage as when she is doing every thing in her power to plague me.[44]

Sheridan frequently employs that made-to-order repartee that was often resorted to by Congreve. It is a kind of wit usually ascribed to the "wittols"; at times, however, even the true wits can not resist making use of it. The audience knows exactly what to expect and yet laughs heartily each time it appears. Sheridan employs this artificial humor in connection with Sir Peter. In one of Sir Peter's habitual squabbles with Lady Teazle, when he is scolding her for incurring so many expenses, there is the following bit of dialogue:

> *Lady Teaz.* Lud, Sir Peter! would you have me be out of the fashion?
> *Sir Pet.* The fashion, indeed! what had you to do with the fashion before you married me?
> *Lady Teaz.* For my part, I should think you would like to have your wife thought a woman of taste.
> *Sir Pet.* Ay—there again—taste! Zounds! madam, you had no taste when you married me![45]

---

[44] II, 1.
[45] II, 1.

Sheridan's method of opening the way for wit is all too obvious, but the humor of the situation brings forth the ready response of the audience, nevertheless.

That Sir Peter Teazle is no fool is indicated in his public denunciation of the "school for scandal," in which he maintains that he would have Parliament enact a law against gossip, permitting only "qualified old maids and disappointed widows"[46] to indulge. His protests are of no avail, however, and he becomes a victim of the "school's" persecution. He has his revenge when his wife resigns from the society to become a dutiful and loving wife. For Sir Peter, also, is reserved the pleasure of ordering the scandalmongers out of his house. Sure of Lady Teazle's love for him, he resolves to control his teasing disposition. In order to accomplish this, he plans to take his wife back to the country, where they will set up an abode far from the eyes of the town fops and gossips.

This solution concludes the amusing study of the elderly bachelor who, much to his own surprise, has won a beautiful young girl for a wife and is faced with the problem of keeping her for himself. The May-and-December situation is an old one, but one which never ceases to be diverting to the audience.

Sheridan's attitude toward the country class was one of tolerant amusement. He satirized them, but did not suggest changes in their mode of life. He portrayed them as he saw them, and he saw them as interesting material for the scrutiny of the artificial London audiences to which he was obliged to cater. Congreve presented the country girl in a most unfavorable light; his Miss Prue exhibits all the undesirable qualities commonly ascribed to the rustic. The country bumpkin was represented by Congreve in his characterization of Sir Wilfull Witwoud, one of Millamant's least successful suitors. Both characters are exaggerations and are indicative of the playwright's aversion to his rural neighbors. Sheridan's country folk are of a different pattern and, apparently, are satirized solely for the humor such treatment always imparts to comic drama.

"Fighting Bob" Acres, a minor rival of Captain Absolute for the hand of Lydia Languish, is typical of Sheridan's method in regard to the country fellow and his awkward attempts to cut a fine figure in London society. He is so earnest in his desire to become

---

[46] II, 2.

a gentleman that he forsakes the familiar hunting-frock and leather breeches for the costume of the city fop; he undertakes to train his hair, since contemporary fashion had decreed the return of natural coiffures; he hires the services of a dancing-master to learn the then popular allemande and cotillion; and, as the final mark of gentility, in his opinion at least, he adopts a curious profanity which he calls "sentimental swearing." His ready analysis of this genteel form of imprecation brings to mind that other detailed scene in *The Critic,* in which Puff, the press-agent, reduces the whole matter of publicity to a science. Acres' delicacy in the choice of oaths is characteristic of the sentimental school, but whether or not it produces the desired effect is doubtful. The reflection upon the language of the genteel comedy is obvious, however; Sheridan could not resist an opportunity which invited comment on this highly affected type of drama. Although Acres' oaths seem to be decidedly lacking in the vituperative strength generally associated with swearing, they can not be criticized in respect to variety. Random examination of the genteel method of imprecation discloses such illuminating examples as "odds frogs and tambours," "odds triggers and flints," "odds whips and wheels," and even "odds blushes and blooms!" Such innovations, thought Acres, threatened to revolutionize the conversation of gentlemen and encourage the art of duelling on a much higher scale!

Through the character of Acres, also, Sheridan makes sport of that popular eighteenth-century pastime—duelling. Ridicule of this business of maintaining one's honor was certainly not original with our playwright. The Restoration, all too obviously influenced by the French in thought, manners, and costumes, mimicked as well the French gallantry which almost invariably resulted in duelling. Like Farquhar, whose dramatic career was noticeably disturbed by his participation in a stage duel, Sheridan was concerned in at least two such encounters with one Mathews, who happened to be in love with Elizabeth Linley. Sheridan could thus reflect with some authority on the folly of this practice, carrying on perhaps the attacks of Richard Steele, who sought anxiously to improve the society of his generation. Sheridan, not so intent upon improving society as upon deriding the system in general, portrayed the clearly unheroic aspects of the duel by having the cowardly Bob Acres as the challenger and the smug, senile Sir Lucius as the manager who instructs Bob in the fine points of duelling, proving that a duel can be fought on no greater provocation than that of a rival's falling in love with one's own beloved. The gullibility of the country lad is, of course, hit upon here when Acres, on the advice of Sir Lucius, actually challenges his rival, Ensign Beverley, to determine which of the two aspirants shall have the lady.

When Acres attempts to justify his action to his man David, a discussion of "honour" ensues which, while echoing the famous Falstaff dissertation, imparts a refreshing touch to the general satire. Just as Acres is deploring the fact that his valor is deserting him, his opponent arrives in the person of Captain Absolute, much to the consternation of Sir Lucius, who is eagerly awaiting the appearance of Ensign Beverley. Acres' joy is without bounds when the Captain reveals that he and Beverley are one and the same person. The realization that he has no reason for quarreling with his good friend Absolute instantly restores his valor and rouses real disgust on the part of Sir Lucius, who calls Acres a coward. Satire on the customary trifles which eighteenth-century men of fashion interpreted as just causes for a duel is found in Acres' response to this insult.

> *Acres.* Look'ee, Sir Lucius, 'tisn't that I mind the word coward—coward may be said in joke—But if you had called me a poltroon, odds daggers and balls—
> *Sir Luc.* Well, sir?
> *Acres.* I should have thought you a very ill-bred man.[47]

Sir Lucius is, accordingly, ready to take on Absolute in an exchange of bullets, but his plans are upset by the timely arrival of Sir Anthony, Mrs. Malaprop, Lydia, and Julia. The differences of all parties concerned are settled amicably at last, and Acres resolves that "if I can't get a wife without fighting for her, by my valour! I'll live a bachelor."[48]

In this way, then, Sheridan presents in caricature his conception of the laughable characteristics of the rustic as they appear in contrast with those of the city fop, and at the same time voices his criticism of duelling in its various aspects. Through the character of Bob Acres he has emphasized the impossibility of disguising the

---

[47] *The Rivals,* V, 3.
[48] V, 3.

earmarks of the country by mere imitation of city fashions; through his treatment of duelling he has held up for ridicule one of the most outstanding foibles of his social class.

CHAPTER III

OSCAR FINGAL O'FLAHERTIE WILLS WILDE

The third dramatist to be considered in this discussion of satire in the comedy of manners is Oscar Wilde.[1] Like Sheridan, he was born in Ireland of upper middle-class parents. His mother was highly regarded in Dublin literary circles and wrote verse under the name "Speranza." The celebrities and literary wits with whom she surrounded herself made Speranza and her salons famous. From her Oscar Wilde inherited two qualities essential to repartee—the love of brilliant conversation and the ability to turn a commonplace into a witticism. His father, knighted for his achievements in the field of eye and ear surgery, acquired further fame by means of the irregularities of his private life, which finally brought him into court to answer seduction charges. From him, perhaps, the son inherited those sexual susceptibilities which were later to cause his downfall. Renier, in his psychological study of Wilde, rightly emphasizes the influence upon the boy Oscar of his childhood environment. Before the birth of this son, "Speranza somehow persuaded herself that it would be a girl. She did not overcome her regret for many years, and continued to dress Oscar in girls' clothes long after the period customary in her day, while she treated him like a girl as long as she possibly could."[2] Renier concludes that although Wilde never was effeminate, he "was a person whose early youth had been such that the feminine side of his psychology had not been eliminated."[3] That Wilde was homosexual is a generally accepted fact. This homosexuality did not, however, prevent his marrying in 1884 Constance Lloyd, by whom he had two sons.

Oscar Wilde's education was the best he could have had. As a boy of nine he was sent to one of the Royal schools of Ireland, where at seventeen he won an Exhibition for Trinity College, Dublin. Although he disliked all manly sports, he was far from unpopular. He was at his best in telling a story and enjoyed nothing more

---

[1] The plays of Wilde on which the discussion in this chapter is based are *Lady Windermere's Fan* (1892), *A Woman of No Importance* (1893), *An Ideal Husband* (1895), and *The Importance of Being Earnest* (1895). The dates are those of presentation.

[2] Renier, G. J., *Oscar Wilde*, p. 23.

[3] *Ibid.*

than holding a group of boys enthralled with the fantastic imaginings of his mind. At Trinity he distinguished himself in the classics, winning a scholarship which enabled him to attend Magdalen College, Oxford. Here he established for himself the reputation of being a scholar, a talker, and an aesthete, the latter distinction being perhaps the most important of all in his life pattern. Oxford gave him Ruskin and Pater, who quickened in him the love of self and beauty which had already set Wilde apart from his fellow students. It was a one-sided development for a scholar—this concentration on "art for art's sake" which Whistler had thrust upon London—for, to Oscar Wilde, the emphasis on cultivation of the mind precluded any necessity for discipline of the body; it was no doubt one of the forces which later led to his deterioration.

In 1878, at the age of twenty-four, Wilde descended upon London as a self-appointed professor of aesthetics and critic of art, and was welcomed warmly by the wealthy and intellectual cliques of society. He gained much notoriety by his adoption of a costume consisting of knee-breeches, silk hose, loose shirt, brightly-colored flowing tie, velvet coat, and velvet beret. His hair he wore shoulder-length, his face he kept clean-shaven, and he generally carried or wore sunflowers or lilies. All this was in keeping with the Whistlerian theory that genius must not be hedged in by convention, and Wilde was convinced of his own genius. His witty phrases and his unconventional dress and actions soon put the name of Oscar Wilde on everyone's lips. This excessive publicity never was of assistance to him financially; his love of aristocratic living led him into so many extravagances that he was almost constantly in debt. In 1891 he created considerable furor with the appearance of his novel, *The Picture of Dorian Gray*. Taken as a whole, it represents the aesthete's creed and contains more expressions of sheer richness and beauty than are commonly found in one volume. In it, too, is mirrored Wilde's passionate admiration for young Lord Alfred Douglas, the Dorian Gray of the book. Wilde turned next to the drama, and in 1892 won recognition for his *Lady Windermere's Fan*. After this success he was certain that his fame lay in play-writing. The next three years brought forth *A Woman of No Importance, An Ideal Husband,* and *The Importance of Being Earnest,* the last being the finest play of all and the one most characteristic of Wilde. Had his career not been unfortunately interrupted by the sordid revelations of the Queensberry trial and his reputation utterly destroyed as a result, he might have continued writing more comedies of manners. Instead, the degradation of the trial weakened the man, leaving him broken in spirit and lacking in ambition. Very soon after he left prison, he went to France, where for the most part his next three years were spent in indolence, solitude, and disillusionment. His jail sentence taught him the value of pity and encouraged him to write the searchingly beautiful *Ballad of Reading Gaol* and *De Profundis,* the latter an exquisite self-revelation in prose. These were the last significant pieces of work he produced. When all efforts toward a reconciliation with his wife failed, Wilde yielded to the irresistible call of Alfred Douglas and Naples, and thereby lost the only bit of self-respect the prison years had left him. Disappointed in Douglas, for whom he had gambled and lost his reputation and career, Wilde returned to Paris, where he rapidly deteriorated.

To Oscar Wilde nothing mattered so much as beauty; it was this particular preoccupation that set him apart from his acquaintances. Ugliness of any kind he despised. In men and women he was constantly seeking physical perfection, and, having once decided that the masculine body most nearly represented his ideals, he was content to ignore the other sex. In life as well as in art he demanded richness of color, symmetry of line, loveliness of touch, and those other attributes of the beautiful which appeal to the senses. In conversation, accordingly, he fashioned beauty out of mere words, moulding and caressing the well-chosen phrase. A great part of the dialogue in his plays was but the perfecting of successful tidbits previously tried out on his friends in casual conversation.

Oscar Wilde was qualified for the business of writing comedies of manners, for he was on familiar terms with fashionable London society at its best and at its worst. He chose his friends as he chose his words—for the pleasure he might derive from them—and because his choice was largely determined by his admiration for the aristocratic life, he was frequently branded a snob. Popularity was his just so long as he kept up the outward semblance of respectability. Even the sophisticated sometimes don a flimsy cloak of morality to satisfy the non-curious and torment the curious; therefore, when Oscar Wilde cast off this hypocritical covering, revealing too clearly his private life, the elite denied him membership in their society and henceforth considered him as an occasional guest or entertainer. Thus, he never experienced the fraternal feeling which had been Congreve's by birth and Sheridan's by invitation. This lack of intimacy was compensated for, however, by the fact that it provided opportunity for viewing the members of this group as a whole.

Wilde's personal appearance often proved a handicap, and even the trappings of the aesthete were of little help in disguising his gigantism, which contrasted so strangely with his feminine coloring and mannerisms. The attractive appearance of both Congreve and Sheridan was to a great extent responsible for their success, whereas Wilde was forced to rely upon his talents alone in order to charm his friends.

Of his two predecessors, Wilde resembles Sheridan more than Congreve, although he has points in common with both. The same clear-cut, metallic combinations of words found in Congreve reappear in Wilde, but Wilde never can compete with him in plot complexity. Both express the same sense of detachment toward their plays. Wilde is in closer contact with Sheridan in regard to his characters and situations. His facile, genial humor is more in keeping with the careless pleasantries of Sheridan than with the calculated wit of Congreve. In cynicism, sophistication, and dexterity of phrase construction, however, Wilde anticipates Noel Coward, and thus ties the comedy of manners of his own day with that of the present.

Satire in Wilde is most frequently expressed by means of the epigram, the paradox, or a similar assembling of striking words and ideas. Often, to be sure, these ingenious quips are utilized for sound rather than for sense, as they were in his conversation, but for the most part they are fairly accurate indications of the writer's thoughts and opinions. Although Wilde makes use of character and situation likewise in developing the satirical, the compact and instantly effective epigram for which he is always remembered is his favorite device.

In Congreve and in Sheridan it was comparatively simple to search out the satire; in Wilde this element becomes suddenly elusive. That the satire is there is a certainty, but its presence is more subtly felt than seen, and for this reason challenges the student to attempt to seek it out and label it accordingly. It appears, in Wilde's writing, in out-of-the-way places where one does not ordinarily expect to find satire. Sometimes it lurks behind a mere phrase or is implied in a single attitude. Very frequently the satirical intent of the writer is revealed in the epigram, which so admirably adapted itself to Wilde's method of expression. For the sake of consistency, it seems desirable to begin the discussion of satire in Oscar Wilde by considering first of all the use he makes of character and situation in the interest of satire.

Wilde appreciated the kind of person he himself professed to be, that is, a worshipper of beauty in all its manifestations who should be at the same time conversant with, and perhaps even superior to, the outstanding figures of his time. One of the prerequisites for such a character he believed to be conversational proficiency, a quality which he had cultivated in himself since childhood and had permitted to dominate his personality. This self-admiration led Wilde, in his novel and in his plays, to model the male characters after himself. At least five men in the four plays we are to consider share in common several attributes peculiar to their author. The men are: John Worthing and Algernon Moncrieff in *The Importance of Being Earnest;* Cecil Graham in *Lady Windermere's Fan;* Lord Goring in *An Ideal Husband;* and Lord Illingworth in *A Woman of No Importance.* All are members of the aristocracy Wilde knew so well and so greatly admired. Perhaps the most distinguishing characteristic is their ability to manufacture provocatively witty and unexpected remarks. The variety of humor prominent in their conversation is the mock-serious, but the presence of it does not import that these gentlemen—and they *are* gentlemen—are incapable of real thought. They are, for the most part, dilettantes to whom the accusation of profligacy is an incidental but unmistakable reflection upon their routine. They are as conceited as Wilde himself was. Generally they show some evidence of artistic talent, often in music, the knowledge of which Wilde always envied in others and pretended to have.

In *An Ideal Husband,* the only play in which Wilde makes use of advance character descriptions, he gives a brief but accurate sketch of Lord Goring which may well be taken as representative of the entire group mentioned above. Lord Goring is:

> *Thirty-four, but always says he is younger. A well-bred, expressionless face. He is clever, but would not like to be thought so. A*

flawless dandy, he would be annoyed if he were considered romantic.
He plays with life, and is on perfectly good terms with the world.
He is fond of being misunderstood. It gives him a post of vantage.[4]

Mabel Chiltern, in a good-humored reply to Lord Caversham, who
alludes to Goring as "my good-for-nothing son," defends the young
man on the grounds that "he rides in the Row at ten o'clock in the
morning, goes to the Opera three times a week, changes his clothes
at least five times a day, and dines out every night of the season."[5]
Much later in the play Wilde comments as follows upon this typical dandy as he presents him in evening dress, the uniform of his
set:

> ....*One sees that he stands in immediate relation to modern life,*
> *makes it indeed, and so masters it. He is the first well-dressed phil-*
> *osopher in the history of thought.*[6]

The portrait is completed by Lord Caversham's hopeless query after
a typical, nonsensical conversation with his son: "Do you always
really understand what you say, sir?" and Goring's calm, respectful
reply: "Yes, father, if I listen attentively."[7]

These excerpts from description and small talk serve as a basis
for discussion, since so much of the satire concerns those characters
which Lord Goring typifies. Actually he is little more than an idealized self-portrait of Oscar Wilde. It is primarily in regard to physical beauty and conventional dress that author and characters part
company. In most other respects one can see Wilde himself through
his characters. Oscar Wilde was innately kind, and Lord Goring is
kind. Both preferred to disguise this quality by an assumed superficiality; both enjoyed shocking their friends by this outward coldness. Even his father repeats over and over again that Goring is
heartless, but Goring was more of a stranger to his father than to
the Chilterns, to whom he proved an invaluable friend.

Like Goring is Cecil Graham, a young man who enjoys conversation of any kind, particularly if it is about himself. It is not very

---

[4] *An Ideal Husband*, I, 158. (Page references for Wilde's plays apply
to the edition of the Book League of America, 1932.)

[5] I, 151.

[6] III, 210.

[7] III, 215.

certain just what is his function in *Lady Windermere's Fan;* it is enough, however, that he is there to lend glitter and verve to an otherwise not very stimulating play. Many of Wilde's sparkling epigrams appear in the repartee of Cecil Graham. The portrait of Graham, though he has not so much seriousness of purpose, is much like that of Goring. Graham talks as Wilde himself talked.

Oscar Wilde frequently tried out certain witticisms and bits of artifice on his friends, and, if they were pleased, he sometimes incorporated these conversational bits into the dialogue of characters like Goring, Graham, or Algy. An instance of such a procedure comes to mind in regard to Graham. Frank Harris records a conversation with Wilde in which Wilde played with the word "lose," as follows:

> "We lose our chances," he [Wilde] said, laughing, "we lose our figures, we even lose our characters; but we must never lose our temper...."[8]

And in *Lady Windermere's Fan* we find Cecil Graham admonishing his friend: "Now, Tuppy, you've lost your figure and you've lost your character. Don't lost your temper; you have only got one."[9]

Most of Graham's amusing remarks are brought about by comments made by others in the group, of whom Lord Augustus—Tuppy to his friends—is the most vulnerable. Attracted by Mrs. Erlynne, Tuppy defends her on the ground that she is not a wicked woman, thus paving the way for Graham's definitive reply: "Wicked women bother one. Good women bore one. That is the only difference between them."[10] Or, again, when Lord Darlington confesses that he loves a married woman, Graham is ready with a bit of paradox: "Well, there's nothing in the world like the devotion of a married woman. It's a thing no married man knows anything about."[11] This was the kind of wit which made Wilde famous.

Like Congreve, Wilde too refined his characters until one in particular became outstanding. The women in Congreve's earlier

---

[8] Harris, Frank, *Oscar Wilde: His Life and Confessions,* p. 97.
[9] *Lady Windermere's Fan,* III, 124.
[10] III, 124.
[11] III, 126.

plays are only foretastes of what appears later in Millamant, a perfect comedy-of-manners heroine. So it is with Wilde. Lord Goring and Cecil Graham eventually lead to the inimitable Algy, who is definitely the comedy-of-manners gentleman. For the duration of *The Importance of Being Earnest,* Algy dominates the action and conversation. Nonsense, one of the most important attributes of sophisticated comedy, reigns supreme in this play. While nonsense depends almost entirely upon artifice for its success, and although it frequently does not follow the logic to which we are accustomed, it can nevertheless convey a certain amount of sense, as is invariably true of Algy's nonsense. The topsy-turviness in this play is comparable only to that which we find later in Noel Coward's comedies, in which the characters are constantly bubbling over with frothy, sparkling repartee. In this play everyone is witty, even Lane, the manservant; but Algy's wit predominates.

The casual, careless existence of the wealthy class fascinated Wilde, but he himself was desirous of a more enduring fame than that derived from idle conversation. It may, accordingly, not be too farfetched to assume that in his frequent depiction of the gallants of this class is a mild criticism of their triviality of purpose.

With the exception of a love affair which develops very conveniently, Algy's concerns are largely those of the professional funster. He is wearing cap and bells at the beginning of the play, and they are evident even at the closing curtain. His tomfoolery ranges from his good-natured attempts to disrupt the romance between his cousin Gwendolyn and his friend Jack, to his posing as Jack's brother for the express purpose of making the acquaintance of Jack's ward, Cecily. While he is engaged in these various pursuits, he manages to toss off many of the epigrams and paradoxes which have long since become common property and still retain their original flavor. Algy's facility at rearranging familiar sayings and thus adding novelty and occasionally more wisdom to them is easily recognized in remarks like the following:

"The very essence of romance is uncertainty."[12]

"Divorces are made in Heaven—"[13]

---

[12] *The Importance of Being Earnest,* I, 5.
[13] I, 5.

Prism. As a model clergyman, he is ever ready to console anyone in time of grief. When Jack Worthing announces the death of his brother Ernest (a brother whom he has invented as a matter of convenience), Dr. Chasuble expresses great sympathy for Jack, and offers to allude to his sorrow on Sunday. He is particularly amusing when he refers to his sermon which can be used on so many different occasions.

> ....My sermon on the meaning of the manna in the wilderness can be adapted to almost any occasion, joyful, or, as in the present case, distressing.... I have preached it at harvest celebrations, christenings, confirmations, on days of humiliation and festal days. The last time I delivered it was in the Cathedral, as a charity sermon on behalf of the Society for the Prevention of Discontentment among the Upper Orders. The Bishop, who was present, was much struck by some of the analogies I drew.[19]

Everything this pompous individual does or says is on a large and ornate scale. A christening assumes with him as great proportions as a mass, and when he talks, he talks in metaphors drawn from the classics and often not very appropriate. Miss Prism, whether she understands the allusions or not, is the only one who duly appreciates him.

In addition to this satire there appears a piece of gossip in *An Ideal Husband* dealing with the marriage of a well-brought-up girl and a curate. It is Lady Markby who comments on the preponderance of curates in contemporary society, particularly country society, a fact which to her seems most irreligious.

Dr. Chasuble, however, is definitely a satire upon the clergy.

There is also an element of satire in Wilde's portrayal of Lane, Algy's manservant, who represents the perfectly-trained man's man. Lane, like his employer, has a good sense of humor and enjoys a joke at any time. His replies to questions addressed to him by Algy, while always polite and deferent, are at the same time witty observations on life, delivered in a sober manner appropriate to his position. In answer to Algy's query as to why at a bachelor's house the servants always drink the champagne, Lane counters with: "I attribute it to the superior quality of the wine, sir. I have often observed that in married households the champagne is rarely of a first-rate

---

[19] II, 36.

brand."[20] And when Algy accuses Lane of being a perfect pessimist, Lane's business-like response is: "I do my best to give satisfaction, sir."[21] The reply does not indicate any misunderstanding
of his employer's statement; it is the facetious comment of an intelligent man who occupies with great assurance his subordinate
position.

Every satirist satirizes gossip and hypocrisy, two of the most
common weaknesses of society. Leisure encourages conversation,
conversation is always accompanied by gossip, and gossip usually
reveals a certain amount of hypocrisy. Oscar Wilde disliked malicious gossip and the people who indulged in it. He himself could
not speak unkindly of anyone, but he did enjoy talking about people,
as is natural for a talker and raconteur. He makes a clear distinction between talking scandal and talking gossip through Cecil Graham, a character much like Wilde, who explains the difference thus:
"Oh, gossip is charming! History is merely gossip. But scandal is
gossip made tedious by morality...."[22] Accordingly, gossip *as* gossip is never satirized by Oscar Wilde. Only when it goes beyond
the bounds of good-natured conversation does he criticize it, as he
does in *Lady Windermere's Fan*. The action of the play, dealing
as it does with the familiar triangle, is brought about by such scandal-mongering, which destroys a faithful wife's implicit trust in her
devoted husband. Here the counterpart of Sheridan's Lady Candour is the Duchess of Berwick. The Duchess' usual source of information is her two nieces, two very domestic creatures who are
"always at the window doing fancy work, and making ugly things
for the poor...."[23] The Duchess may be taken as a representative
of all the ladies in society who thrive on stories involving other people's reputations. She is like them also in regard to hypocrisy. She
joins with the others in disparaging the character of Mrs. Erlynne,
the woman with whom, to all outward appearances, the very proper
Lord Windermere is involved. When she meets Mrs. Erlynne at
Lady Windermere's ball, however, she is at once ready to accept her
and to discredit the rumors of her nieces. Mrs. Erlynne is a woman
of the world and knows that the way to get back into respectable

---

[20] *The Importance of Being Earnest*, I, 27.
[21] I, 27.
[22] *Lady Windermere's Fan*, III, 125.
[23] I, 88.

society is through just such an invitation. Her wisdom in this respect becomes more evident when the discriminating guests shower her with more invitations than she cares for. The fact that even the Bishop is to be present at one luncheon is a certain stamp of approval.

Examples of the harmless gossip which Wilde tolerated and in which he often participated are to be found in *An Ideal Husband,* in the conversation of Lady Markby, who talks about people solely for the sake of talking. She has no real intention of wounding the persons of whom she speaks, but discusses them because they are subjects about whom she can be facetious. Such gossip is the basis of successful conversation and repartee.

Since there is nothing particularly attractive about spinster-hood, and since Wilde's creed insisted upon the beautiful in all phases of life, there is justification for his burlesque treatment of Miss Prism, the governess in *The Importance of Being Earnest.* According to Lady Bracknell, Miss Prism is "a female of repellent aspect, remotely connected with education," while, according to Dr. Chasuble, she is "the most cultivated of ladies, and the very picture of respectability."[24] Which of the two portraits is the accurate one is questionable, since Lady Bracknell thinks of Miss Prism only as a servant, while the good canon considers the governess one of the most attractive members of his congregation. She has pretensions to learning, and has, in fact, written a three-volume novel. She takes more than a friendly interest in Dr. Chasuble and is trying to encourage a reciprocal interest in him. Miss Prism is always flattered when he addresses any metaphorical references to her, for she considers his conversation an indirect compliment upon her own education. Her attempts to equal his forced and rather farfetched metaphors are ludicrous. She gives even Dr. Chasuble quite a start when she refers to young women as green fruit, and is very careful to explain that she is speaking horticulturally. Her methods in regard to matrimony can hardly be termed subtle, but Dr. Chasuble seems willing to be ensnared. Her argument is that "by persistently remaining single, a man converts himself into a permanent public temptation. Men should be careful; this very celibacy leads weaker vessels astray."[25] The embrace at the end

---

[24] *The Importance of Being Earnest,* III, 69.
[25] II, 34.

of the play seems to indicate that Dr. Chasuble is entertaining serious misgivings concerning the problem of celibacy, a situation which may be chalked up as a definite victory for Miss Prism.

Further bits of satire on old maids are to be found in the comments of the Duchess of Berwick about her gossipy nieces who have nothing better to do than to sit at the window and concoct scandalous tales for circulation.[26]   In Miss Prism, however, Wilde has given an amusing as well as realistic picture of spinsterhood.

To criticize society one does not necessarily have to be a pessimist.   The optimist or the middle-of-the-way man can do the job just as well.   All that is required is keen insight into the ways of men, a good sense of humor, and ready wit.   Oscar Wilde was born with all these qualities and readily adopted criticism of his social class as a major purpose in his life.   He had very little, if any, intention of reforming his fellow men.   His was a more egotistic purpose which aimed at self-satisfaction primarily.   When he called attention to the foibles of society, he did so, not with the gloomy attitude of the prophet who forecasts disaster, but with the contented outlook of the man who welcomes the disillusioning aspects of life as well as its virtues.   Above all, his well-turned comments gave Wilde the added pleasure of rousing his listeners out of their usual complacency.

There was much in the continual comedy of manners going on about him that deserved ridicule, and Oscar Wilde indulged fully his discerning sense of the satirical.   Although he liked to be associated with the aristocratic section of society, he could nevertheless reflect upon the idiosyncrasies of a class which set up property, wealth, and influential connections as restrictions upon its membership.   There is the famous scene in *The Importance of Being Earnest* wherein Lady Bracknell catechizes Jack Worthing, her daughter's suitor, regarding his eligibility.   Such emphasis is laid upon the very trivial in this interview that the result is delightful satire upon the requisites of this exclusive clan.   Thus, we are not surprised at Lady Bracknell's first inquiry, "Do you smoke?" or at her observation upon Jack's affirmative reply: "I am glad to hear it.   A man should always have an occupation of some kind.   There are far too many idle men in London as it is...."[27]   Her frank

---

[26] *Lady Windermere's Fan*, I, 88.
[27] *The Importance of Being Earnest*, I, 19.

questions regarding his income, investments, and even politics are particularly amusing, accompanied as they are by numerous jottings in her notebook. In typical topsy-turvy, Wildean fashion, she inquires about his parents:

> *Lady Bracknell.* ...Now to minor matters. Are your parents living?
> *Jack.* I have lost both my parents.
> *Lady Bracknell.* Both?...That seems like carelessness. Who was your father? He was evidently a man of some wealth. Was he born in what the Radical papers call the purple of commerce, or did he rise from the ranks of the aristocracy?[28]

When Jack reveals that he was found in a black leather handbag in the cloak-room at Victoria Station, Lady Bracknell pronounces judgment to the effect that a cloak-room can "hardly be regarded as an assured basis for a recognized position in good society,"[29] and advises Jack to produce at least one parent before she will consider him. Jack's offer to produce the handbag meets with great indignation and brings to a close the unsatisfactory interview, for, as Lady Bracknell states, "You can hardly imagine that I and Lord Bracknell would dream of allowing our only daughter—a girl brought up with the utmost care—to marry into a cloak-room, and form an alliance with a parcel? Good morning, Mr. Worthing!"[30]

In this almost farcical scene is to be found much of Wilde's attitude toward the false values of society. The frivolousness of the diagolue is not simply for theatrical effect, but serves to accentuate an underlying seriousness of thought regarding hypocritical class standards.

Perhaps the closest revelation of Wilde's real opinion of society appears in *A Woman of No Importance*. Gerald Arbuthnot has just been appointed secretary to Lord Illingworth, who, although Gerald does not know it, is his father. Gerald is anxious to follow in his employer's footsteps and questions him about society.

> *Gerald.* But it is very difficult to get into society, isn't it?
> *Lord Illingworth.* To get into the best society, nowadays, one has either to feed people, amuse people, or shock people—that is all.

[28] I, 20.
[29] I, 21.
[30] I, 22.

> *Gerald.* I suppose society is wonderfully delightful!
> *Lord Illingworth.* To be in it is merely a bore. But to be out
> of it simply a tragedy. Society is a necessary thing....[31]

Oscar Wilde was qualified to speak on the uses of society, for his experiences in this regard were many and varied. He spent his money, his ambition, and his talents in catering to an unappreciative social clique which wanted only to be amused. As Osbert Burdett observes, "It was remarkable, and must have seemed ironical to himself, that a man so much talked of should have found no reward for his gifts except a succession of invitations to dinner."[32] Again and again we find Wilde calling attention to society. There is Lady Bracknell's warning to her nephew: "Never speak disrespectfully of society, Algernon. Only people who can't get into it do that...."[33] There is Mabel Chiltern's discovery that London society is made up of "beautiful idiots and brilliant lunatics. Just what society should be."[34] And there is Lord Caversham's conviction that London society "has gone to the dogs, a lot of damned nobodies talking about nothing."[35] There are numerous similar remarks with which Wilde liked to prod this inert company with which he himself was affiliated.

A question on which Oscar Wilde was always eloquent was marriage. This was only to be expected of a man who was allowed to reign over the conversation of the elite, whose table-talk invariably deals with the relationships of men and women. As is always the case in the comedy of manners, anything suggesting convention and respectability is derided in conversation, no doubt because the majority of persons who indulge in such conversation are at heart quite conventional and respectable. It is simply an unwritten code among the sophisticated that one's real opinions on life, if they are at all ordinary, must never be disclosed in public and seldom, if ever, in private. Such a prohibition, while not mandatory, adds zest to the repartee, which, where marriage is concerned, becomes unusally sparkling and flippant. For Oscar Wilde such an attitude toward anything at all provided innumerable opportunities for paradoxi-

---

[31] *A Woman of No Importance,* III, 301.
[32] Burdett, Osbert, *The Beardsley Period,* p. 134.
[33] *The Importance of Being Earnest,* III, 65.
[34] *An Ideal Husband,* I, 151.
[35] I, 160.

cal statements which never failed to entertain the crowd. His knack for turning upside down familiar phrases or proverbs was a disturbing one, particularly because very often the result contained as much truth and sense as the original. He plays with the question of respectable marriages when he has Algy say: "The amount of women in London who flirt with their own husbands is perfectly scandalous. It looks so bad. It is simply washing one's clean linen in public."[36] Just a few remarks later, Algy rearranges one of our most familiar proverbs to say that "in married life three is company and two is none."[37] Dialogue such as this indicates an original outlook rather than mere smartness on the part of Oscar Wilde.

Those who are married are in a better position to jest about marital relationships and romance, and this fact gives Wilde many occasions for the epigrammatic. Accordingly, we find Mrs. Allonby, one of the most sophisticated of Wilde's characters, conversing thus with Lord Illingworth:

> *Mrs. Allonby.* I should have thought Lady Caroline would have grown tired of conjugal anxiety by this time! Sir John is her fourth!
> *Lord Illingworth.* So much marriage is certainly not becoming. Twenty years of romance make a woman look like a ruin; but twenty years of marriage make her something like a public building.
> *Mrs. Allonby.* Twenty years of romance! Is there such a thing?[38]

Finally there is Lord Illingworth's pronouncement regarding grounds for marriage: "Men marry because they are tired; women because they are curious. Both are disappointed."[39]

Wilde also enjoyed satirizing arranged marriages. His own had been a marriage of convenience—he needed money, and Constance Lloyd had a little to offer. It is doubtful whether real love entered into the transaction, if one is to judge from later events in his life.

The most memorable "take-off" on arranged marriages is found in *The Importance of Being Earnest,* and emphasizes an attitude common to Wilde and Sheridan. That the comedy of man-

[36] *The Importance of Being Earnest,* I, 11.
[37] I, 11.
[38] *A Woman of No Importance,* I, 270.
[39] III, 302.

ners, dealing over and over again as it does with the same class of
people set up against differing backgrounds of time and current
events, should repeat itself in regard to characterization is not unexpected, and again and again we meet our old friends in new dress.
We have noted to some extent the evolution of the ladies and gallants from Millamant and Mirabell to Lydia Languish and Captain
Absolute; their lineal descendants now appear in Mabel Chiltern
and Lord Goring, in Algy Montcrieff and Cecily, and in Jack (Ernest) Worthing and Gwendolyn.   Perhaps the closest kinship
exists between Captain Absolute and Goring, a kinship extending
even to their fathers—Sir Anthony Absolute and Lord Caversham.
Both young men are typical of the comedy of manners in their
savoir faire and their obvious pursuit of the trivial.   Anyone reading or watching the scene between Lord Goring and his father, in
which Lord Caversham tries to persuade his son to marry, must
recall the very similar scene between Captain Absolute and his
father in *The Rivals*.   In each instance the father bungles the
business of arranging a marriage for the son, who displays the
customary affected disrespect for parental authority. Captain Absolute, to be sure, has reason for permitting himself to be intimidated,
since he has been threatened with disinheritance and since he suspects that the woman his father would have him marry is none other
than Lydia, whom he already loves.   Goring, too, is directed to
take a wife of his father's choosing, for, as Lord Caversham points
out: "There is property at stake.   It is not a matter for affection.
Affection comes later on in married life."[40]   In both situations the
satire is on arranged marriages and the parents who attempt to ar-
range them.   Apparently there is also intended a reflection upon
the materialistic attitude of the sophisticated with regard to the
distinction they make between love and mere marital relationships.

Lady Bracknell's interview with Jack Worthing, mentioned
previously, is a case in point.   Another, Wilde's portrayal of the
scheming Duchess of Berwick and her marriageable daughter Agatha, provides comic relief in a play conspicuous for its melodramatic
presentation of an idealistic wife and her reactions to gossip about
her husband.   As for Agatha, it is fortunate that she has someone
to make the necessary manoeuvers for her, since she is one of those

---

[40] *An Ideal Husband*, III, 218.

helpless creatures who are brought up in complete ignorance of the life going on about them. She has no opinions and, consequently, nothing to say. Her conversation is limited to an occasional "Yes, Mamma." The characterization is an exaggerated but merited reflection upon parents who regulate too closely the lives of their children, thus depriving them of any individuality they may have had. The machinations of the Duchess of Berwick finally result in the capture of an Australian husband for Agatha. The most effective lines are those relating to Agatha's acceptance of Mr. Hopper's proposal.

> *Duchess of Berwick.* Agatha, darling! (*Beckons her over.*)
> *Lady Agatha.* Yes, Mamma!
> *Duchess of Berwick.* (*aside.*) Did Mr. Hopper definitely—
> *Lady Agatha.* Yes, Mamma.
> *Duchess of Berwick.* And what answer did you give him, dear child?
> *Lady Agatha.* Yes, Mamma.
> *Duchess of Berwick* (*affectionately*). My dear one! You always say the right thing....[41]

Indications that Oscar Wilde thought not too highly of the education of the upper class, crop up occasionally. In general it is true that the higher strata of society find education in itself a rather negligible factor in the upbringing of youth, and consider a more liberal acquaintance with the social graces of greater value in fitting them for the positions they will occupy later. In a very casual manner Wilde has Lady Bracknell comment upon the subject:

> ... The whole theory of modern education is radically unsound. Fortunately in England, at any rate, education produces no effect whatsoever. If it did, it would prove a serious danger to the upper classes, and probably lead to violence in Grosvenor Square.[42]

At a ball in Grosvenor Square, in *An Ideal Husband,* two very decorative and sophisticated ladies come to the conclusion that being educated "puts one almost on a level with the commercial classes."[43] This is, of course, mere jesting on the part of the characters and

---

[41] *Lady Windermere's Fan,* II, 109.
[42] *The Importance of Being Earnest,* I, 19.
[43] *An Ideal Husband,* I, 149.

Wilde, but conveyed in the remarks is a semi-seriousness which suggests rather than states that the education of the superior class is after all superficial.

On the subject of America and Americans, Oscar Wilde had much to say. In 1882, ten years before he wrote *A Woman of No Importance,* he went on a lecture tour through the leading cities in America. According to Frank Harris, Wilde announced through his brother's newspaper that he had been invited to lecture in America because of the success of his first published poems.[44] Another story has it that the tour was sponsored by a firm of London tailors. Whichever story sounds more probable, it is a fact that Wilde was in great need of money, and the lectures seemed a fairly promising financial venture. As it actually turned out, Wilde's profits were very slight and soon dwindled away in characteristic fashion. In America, Wilde visited every section of the United States and Canada. Except in a few less appreciative cities, of which Bangor, Maine, was an example, his audiences were large, drawn together for the most part by curiosity, but generally won over before the close of his instructive lectures by the sincerity of the speaker. Stoically he endured the ridicule of the American press and the notoriety that had already preceded him, including the caricature of himself in Gilbert and Sullivan's *Patience,* which was still being presented in the United States.

Wilde's was not a spiteful nature, and his attacks on America and on American manners are very mild indeed. The few bits of satire on America appear in *A Woman of No Importance,* notably in the character of Hester Worsley, a young woman visiting in England. Hester's father made his fortune in American dry goods, which Lord Illingworth defines as American novels.[45] Her well-dressed appearance is attributed to the fact that all Americans get their clothes in Paris.[46] Lord Illingworth's banter includes one of Wilde's most famous epigrams. Mr. Kelvil, a serious member of Parliament, feels he must defend America, and thus gives the cue for the familiar commentary.

---

[44] *Op. cit.,* p. 51.
[45] *A Woman of No Importance,* I, 264.
[46] I, 264.

> *Kelvil.* I am afraid you don't appreciate America, Lord Illing-
> worth. It is a very remarkable country, especially considering its
> youth.
>   *Lord Illingworth.* The youth of America is their oldest tradi-
> tion. It has been going on now for three hundred years. To hear
> them talk one would imagine they were in their first childhood. As
> far as civilization goes they are in their second.[47]

Unless the reader, too, is a puritan, he does not like Hester very
much. She is too righteous and patriotic to mix well with the sophisticated, liberal English smart set, and although she is an attractive young lady, she is not very pleasant company. Her outspokenness comes as a surprise to the other guests, but is passed off as a
purely American characteristic. The contrast between Hester and
the worldly Mrs. Allonby is great, since each despises what the
other stands for. Hester's mission seems to be to spread the gospel
of morality and Americanism; Mrs. Allonby's is an iconoclastic one
which ridicules the conventional and embraces the unusual. Although her hostess and guests allow Hester to harangue them with
her ideas of what is right and wrong with English society, it is quite
evident that her words are falling on deaf ears. Mrs. Allonby is
extremely bored. As Lord Illingworth says, "All Americans lecture, I believe. I suppose it is something in their climate."[48] After
spending most of her time in damning the immorality of this society
and demanding equal punishment for the sinners and the sinned
against, Hester marries Gerald Arbuthnot, the illegitimate son of
Mrs. Arbuthnot and Lord Illingworth, and thus violates all her best
principles.

Hester Worsley represented for Oscar Wilde the qualities he
disliked in American women, and by placing such a character in
the midst of a group which prides itself upon its disregard of the
serious things in life, he accordingly achieves the satirical purpose.
One feels almost like an accessory before the fact at hearing Lord
Illingworth accept Mrs. Allonby's challenge to kiss the puritan.
The truth of the matter is, however, that one can not really enjoy
the comedy of manners and admire Hester Worsley at the same
time.

---

[47] I, 265.
[48] II, 290.

Oscar Wilde's satire of the puritan was not confined to the American Hester Worsley, but extended to English women as well, as is readily seen in the characterizations of two important women, Lady Chiltern, in *An Ideal Husband,* and Lady Windermere, in *Lady Windermere's Fan.* Both are very useful for the sake of contrast, since their continual concentration upon what is right and what is wrong is at odds with the general attitudes of their social set.

Lady Chiltern is a woman of the highest moral principles and has no sympathy for those who do not share them. She has been fortunate enough to marry a man of seemingly impeccable character, one of the most influential members of Parliament. Sir Robert Chiltern is a model husband, whom one would never suspect of doing anything dishonorable. Lady Chiltern, for this reason more than for any other, has idealized her husband to such an extent that she can not bring herself to believe that his career has been built upon a great scandal, an eighteen-year-old secret which is on the verge of being exposed. Like Hester, Lady Chiltern, too, finally comes to the conclusion that love is a greater factor in life than mere moral perfection, a decision which leads to a deeper understanding of human weaknesses and a reconciliation with Sir Robert. Lady Markby, a good judge of character, wisely observes that "Lady Chiltern has a very ennobling effect on life, though her dinner-parties are rather dull sometimes."[49] Unalleviated morality, while protective on the whole, is never very interesting or exciting for either the moralist or the observer.

The other puritan, Lady Windermere, attempts to account for her own uprightness:

> ....I lived always with Lady Julia, my father's eldest sister, you know. She was stern to me, but she taught me, what the world is forgetting, the difference that there is between what is right and what is wrong. *She* allowed of no compromise. *I* allow of none.[50]

Like the other two ladies, she condemns moral laxness of any kind. She refuses to invite to her house any person whose name has been linked with scandal, a restriction which she finds is more easily laid

[49] *An Ideal Husband,* I, 172.
[50] *Lady Windermere's Fan,* I, 82.

down with regard to women than to men. Again, one wonders how she manages to get along as well as she does with her sophisticated friends. Lady Windermere's position is very similar to Lady Chiltern's in that she too has married a pattern husband, whom she believes incapable of indiscretion until his name becomes involved with that of Mrs. Erlynne, a woman of questionable reputation. The situation is a trite and melodramatic one. Mrs. Erlynne is the mother of Lady Windermere, but the secret is divulged only to Lord Windermere and the audience. It is interesting to note that the man to whom Lady Windermere turns, when she hears the story about her husband and Mrs. Erlynne, is Lord Darlington, a man who meets few if any of the puritan requirements. It is not until Mrs. Erlynne saves her daughter from running away with Lord Darlington that Lady Windermere realizes the innate goodness of the woman she had hitherto looked upon as a wicked influence upon society. Through Mrs. Erlynne, Lady Windermere learns that the standards she had set up for herself and her husband are hypocritical ones, and once again love triumphs over all.

Wilde was not so much concerned with pointing out a moral as he was with depicting cross sections of society as he saw it. To him, moral rectitude as displayed in the characters of the puritan ladies he characterized, is quite as harmful to any social order as is immorality. There is a great deal of truth in Lord Darlington's estimate of goodness: "Do you know I am afraid that good people do a great deal of harm in this world. Certainly the greatest harm they do is that they make badness of such extraordinary importance."[51]

With regard to the intriguing Mrs. Cheveleys and Mrs. Erlynnes the observation of Lady Plymdale must be mentioned, because its cynicism is so characteristic of Wilde. Her comment is that "women of that kind are most useful. They form the basis of other people's marriages."[52] This comment expresses quite adequately Wilde's attitude toward the "other women." It was not a matter in which he was much concerned, for, like other members of the smart set, he was little bothered by marital infidelity or even fidelity. Anything or anyone enriching for him the experiences of

---

[51] I, 83.
[52] II, 106.

ordinary life was of interest to him and worthy of inclusion in his writing and conversation.   Thus, although we find Mrs. Cheveley and Mrs. Erlynne occupying prominent positions in his plays, we must not consider them as objects of satire primarily; they represent a very important sector of the society Wilde was satirizing on the whole.

CHAPTER IV

NOEL COWARD

Of contemporary writers of the comedy of manners in the tradition of Congreve, Sheridan, and Wilde, the one who has perhaps best captured the spirit of his generation is Noel Coward.[1] He was born at Teddington, not far from London, on December 16, 1899, the son of Arthur Coward and Violet Veitch. In his youth he obtained an intimate familiarity with the theatre which has since made his name generally associated with theatrical excellence. This introduction came through his parents and other members of the Coward family, which he has described as "enormous, active, and fiercely musical."[2] Among the many dramatic and musical activities in which his father and mother took part were some associated with St. Albans Church, in which the boy's services were early enlisted. Although he managed to win prizes in amateur singing and dancing competitions, he failed in an audition for the Chapel Royal choir. This defeat, however, turned him back to the theatre; and at the age of nine, after many small triumphs at local concerts and garden parties, he became a member of a provincial repertory company and made his acting debut in London, in a children's play, *The Goldfish*. Incidentally, another member of this company was Gertrude Lawrence, who later was to play opposite Coward in *Private Lives* and in several of his most recent productions. This first stage appearance pointed for the child-actor Noel the way to a succession of minor parts in such plays as *Peter Pan* and *Little Lord Fauntleroy*. While yet in his teens, he joined the Liverpool Repertory Theatre and acted in *Hannele*. A little later he was at the head of a barnstorming company presenting the well-known farce *Charley's Aunt*. In the last year of the World War he served for a short time in the army. In 1920 he was back on the stage again, performing in Beaumont and Fletcher's *The Knight of the Burning Pestle*.

It was in 1920 that his first play, *I'll Leave It to You*, was pro-

---

[1] The plays of Noel Coward on which the discussion in this chapter is based are *The Vortex* (1923), *Hay Fever* (1925), *Easy Virtue* (1926), *Private Lives* (1930), *Design for Living* (1933), and *Point Valaine* (1935). The dates are those of presentation.

[2] Coward, Noel, *Present Indicative*, p. 5.

duced. This is a very light comedy describing a family of well-born young people who are suddenly confronted with the business of supporting themselves. In the same year he made his first visit to America, where he attracted cordial attention from a limited group. *I'll Leave It to You* was followed by two unimportant plays, *The Young Idea,* a satire on English county society, and *The Rat Trap,* a treatment of the conflicting problems of two literary-minded persons who happen to be married to each other. These plays provided the necessary practice work. Not until the presentation of *The Vortex,* however, in 1923, did Noel Coward actually come into his own as a playwright.

Since 1920, Mr. Coward has been amazingly and successfully prolific. The most disconcerting fact about him is the astounding facility with which he can turn out play after play. One can never be very accurate in estimating the number of plays he has written because while one is in the process of jotting down an approximate figure, along comes a press notice to the effect that Noel Coward has done it again. For example, at the close of 1935, *Point Valaine* brought the total number of his plays and revues to twenty-three. With the turn of the new year came the announcement that there were nine new Coward offerings, and that the playwright intended to dispose of them three at a time in one week at the Phoenix Theatre, London. The plays, under the inclusive title *Tonight at 8:30,* were presented in New York during the 1936-37 season, with Noel Coward and Gertrude Lawrence in the leading roles, and were extremely successful. Each group is enough varied within itself to provide a well-rounded evening's entertainment, while the entire cycle, for those who can afford the triple set-up, is a stimulating and original contribution to the theatre. The approximate number of Mr. Coward's plays and revues is, accordingly, thirty-two at present, although tomorrow or next week or next month may add still another to this impressive list.

His multitudinous talents, which with each play become more and more evident, have earned for Noel Coward such titles as the "superman of the theatre" and the "modern theatre's wonder boy." John Mason Brown, in his delightful series of letters from "greenroom ghosts" to their present-day successors, through the character of Sheridan summarizes and lauds Mr. Coward's versatility:

As a performer, your equipment is such that you can add as much
gaiety to a madcap turn in a revue as neurotic tension to a tragedy
of post-war nerves, or high polish to a sophisticated comedy. As a
writer, your pen has proven itself as hospitable to romance as it is to
cynicism, to tragedy as to nonsense, to patter as to prose, to farce as
to melodrama, to plays as to revues, to operettas as to comedies, to
rough-and-tumble burlesques as to sentimental lyrics, and to the patri-
otism of such a stirring pageant of empire as *Cavalcade* as it is to the
pacifism that not only vents its hatred of war but that condemns the
futility of sacrifice in the bitter pages of *Post Mortem.* You can sing
and dance acceptably, play the piano with ease, write charming melo-
dies for the scores of your own musical comedies, invent dance steps
for the chorus numbers you may want to use, and direct your own
productions with the virtuoso's touch you brought to the staging of
Cavalcade....[3]

To this long list of achievements should be added still another—his
successful debut in moving pictures in 1935 as the leading character
in Ben Hecht and Charles MacArthur's study of the super-cynical,
egoistic, heartless publisher, in *The Scoundrel.* In March, 1937,
Noel Coward completed his autobiography, on which he had been
writing for three years. Although written in the usual "Coward
style," so frequently labelled superficial, it reveals a surprising
seriousness of purpose. One is never allowed to forget that his
greatest passion is for the theatre, and that his own life and all the
world about him are accounted for in terms of it.

Mr. Coward's meteoric rise to success has revealed to his public not just another famous playwright but a distinguished and fascinating personality. Although he is not a handsome man, he makes
a decidedly pleasing appearance and may easily be taken as the pro-
totype for any one of the several sophisticated gentlemen he has
created in his plays. He acts and talks like them, is nonchalant of
manner, witty in conversation, and worldly in outlook. Like Congreve, he too is a member of the society he depicts in his writing,
and for that reason can take liberties in disclosing their manners
and frailties.

There have been many attempts on both sides of the Atlantic
to write plays in the Coward style, but these self-conscious efforts
never quite measure up to his seemingly casual achievements. Sar-
torially speaking, he has done a great deal toward popularizing for-

---

[3] Brown, John Mason, *Letters from Greenroom Ghosts,* p. 137.

mal evening clothes for men, the uniform of the smart set, and has
been hailed by authorities on male attire as one of the best-dressed
men of the day. His frequent trips tò America have made him a
welcome visitor here, while the newspapers have long since discov-
ered his publicity value. The Walter Winchells and the O. O. Mc-
Intyres are necessarily indebted to Mr. Coward, for he is such stuff
as newspaper columns are made on. His witty and amusing remarks, like those of Wilde, are constantly being quoted and mis-
quoted; he has even been travestied in a musical comedy, *As Thou-
sands Cheer,* by Irving Berlin and Moss Hart. For the last lines
of *Cavalcade*—the toast to England expressing the hope that "this
country of ours, which we love so much, will find dignity and great-
ness and peace again,"—were substituted the parody: "Here's to
Noel Coward. May he find happiness and peace and dignity again!"

In his informal but very valuable introduction to the latest
collection of his most representative plays, the dramatist expresses
his opinion that "a professional writer should be animated by no
other motive than the desire to write, and, by doing so, to earn his
living."[4] That Mr. Coward has the desire to write is a fact which
the very number and frequency of his plays make obvious, but for
the most part he permits it to manifest itself only in delineation of
his particular social set. He is not a moralist and has no idea of
reforming the members of this set. His object is to give a realistic
portrayal of one section of contemporary life. It so happens that
this section, with all its sophistication, its cultivation of smart talk,
and its concentration upon nonchalance and gayety, lends itself
admirably to satire. The playwright's treatment of these weaknesses and flippancies does not indicate that he disapproves of his
contemporaries; it merely implies that he is capable of detaching
himself from them long enough to present in a convincing manner
their "slice of life."

Mr. Coward has been much more experimental than any of
the other three playwrights already discussed; he has tried his hand
at revues, operettas, patriotic pieces, and plays overflowing with
sentiment and emotion. But more consistently he has adhered to
the comedy of manners as we are most familiar with it—clearly-
etched studies of the life of the smart set. Since these are Coward's

---

[4] Coward, Noel, *Play Parade,* Introduction, p. viii.

most characteristic work, it has seemed advisable to select for the purposes of this discussion the comedies in this group which are most notable for the satirical element in them. The list, accordingly, has been narrowed down to *The Vortex, Hay Fever, Easy Virtue, Private Lives, Design for Living,* and *Point Valaine.*

Noel Coward has achieved an enviable position in the theatre world, and as so often happens with celebrated dramatists, has been idolized by his audiences and victimized by the critics. Mr. Coward, however, is too well versed in the ways of the theatre to forget that what really matters is the line at the box office and not the iconoclastic holders of the complimentary tickets.

Noel Coward has been very influential in the matter of dialogue. The conversations of his characters are not what might have been said, but what ordinarily would have been said. He has an unusual knack for reproducing dialogue which in its naturalness is particularly convincing and difficult to imitate. In addition to this ability, he has an extraordinary sense of what is and what is not good theatre, as well as excellent judgment concerning theatre technique in general. Somerset Maugham vests in this young playwright a great responsibility when he states that "since there is no one now writing who has more obviously a gift for the theatre than Mr. Noel Coward, nor more influence with young writers, it is probably his inclination and practice that will be responsible for the manner in which plays will be written during the next twenty years."[5]

The people of whom Noel Coward writes appear to differ slightly from the ones in whom Congreve, Sheridan, and Wilde were interested. They are not members of the aristocracy, although they do comprise the upper crust of a fashionable society which, in keeping with the times, has exchanged the claims of nobility for those of wealth. In addition, particularly in England, as Cunliffe points out, "the place of the older landowners has been largely taken by the new rich, who adopt the amusements of their predecessors without assuming their duties, for which they substitute the excitements and excesses of city life."[6] Actually there is no real difference. The titles of the nobility which formerly gave sanction to

---

[5] Coward, Noel, *Bitter Sweet and Other Plays,* Introduction, p. vii.
[6] Cunliffe, John W., *Modern English Playwrights,* p. 230.

their indulgences and weaknesses are lacking, but the familiar figures of the comedy of manners are plainly recognizable. It is this class, the idle sophisticated set of today, which attracts the attention of Noel Coward.

The Vortex, written when Coward was only twenty-four, reveals much impatience on the part of the author with the perpetual striving of its characters for relief from their cultivated boredom. Because it was written such a short time after 1918 and thus has an occasional allusion to the war, and because it represented characters with frayed nerves, critics early fell into the habit of referring to Mr. Coward as a playwright dealing solely with post-war hysteria, psychoanalysis, and jazz. Mr. Coward's main concern in writing *The Vortex,* according to his own statement, was that of writing a play "with a whacking good part in it for myself."[7] Any observations which bear reference to or show results of the war must, therefore, be discounted as background incidentals.

In addition to the "whacking good part" he wrote for himself, Mr. Coward created one or two others of equal excellence, notably that of Florence Lancaster. The satirical element is obvious throughout this characterization of the middle-aged woman who, going on the vain assumption that she is still young, continues to take unto herself youthful lovers. It is evident from the outset that she will not be successful in her affair with Tom Veryan; middle-aged women seldom are. Florence's situation is a complicated one, since the girl to whom she loses the lover is engaged to Florence's son Nicky.

It is about Florence's vanity that the whole play fluctuates, and when her vanity seems finally undermined by the denunciation of her own son, the play arrives at its somewhat equivocal conclusion. Florence represents the typical woman of her class. She has no responsibilities. Her son she has neglected for years, and she no longer understands him; her husband exists somewhere in her vicinity, but she is practically oblivious of the fact. Occasionally she is reminded by her friends that she is neglecting her husband and son, but her response is always the same:

---

[7] *Play Parade,* Introduction, p. x.

> I'm devoted to David—I'd do anything for him, anything in the
> world—but he's grown old and I've kept young; it does muddle things
> up so. I can't help having a temperament, can I?[8]

And with this declaration Florence feels she has done her duty
toward her family. She has no use for friends as such, and for this
reason rebukes Helen, a friend of the family, who attempts to criticize her manner of living. Helen, apparently having more common
sense than anyone else in the play, does not hesitate to tell Florence
the truth whenever she is moved to do so. Helen's theory is that
"it's silly not to grow old when the time comes,"[9] but for Florence,
who intends to be young indefinitely, the words have no meaning.
Florence is a pathetic rather than a sympathetic character, and thus
is more suitable for the satire implied. Not brilliant enough to
stand out as an individual in a society where the shams are so numerous, she thinks that her concentration on self makes her a social
asset. Nicky, who has inherited most of his mother's selfish qualities, understands her best of all and finds himself justifying her actions before Bunty, his fiancée:

> . . . . She is terribly silly about being "young," I know, but she's been
> used to so much admiration and flattery and everything always, she
> feels she sort of can't give it up—you do see that, don't you? And she
> hasn't really anything in the least comforting to fall back upon. She's
> not clever—real kind of brain cleverness—and father's no good, and
> I'm no good, and all the time she's wanting life to be as it was instead
> of as it is. There's no harm in her anywhere—she's just young in-
> side. Can't you imagine the utter foulness of growing old? . . . .[10]

Nicky is aware of the vacuousness of their lives, but has himself
degenerated to such an extent that he does not care to do anything
about it. Not until Nicky announces that Bunty is on her way to
meet his mother does even a momentary shudder of parental responsibility come over Florence, but it instantly gives way to the more
important question as to whether or not Bunty will like *her*. As
soon as she learns that Bunty and Tom Veryan are old friends,
Florence becomes jealous, eventually making a fool of herself when

---

[8] *The Vortex*, I, 439. (Page references for this play apply to *Play Parade*, Doubleday, Doran and Company, Inc., 1933.)

[9] I, 441.

[10] II, 474.

she discovers Tom making love to the girl. It is the old story of age versus youth, and as usual youth wins out. The seriousness of the situation is twofold here, however, for when Florence loses her lover, Nicky is similarly bereft.

More than the characterization of the selfish Florence, that of her son Nicky makes the tone of the play decidedly unpleasant. Nicky is a young man of considerable musical talent, intelligence, and attraction, and in a decent environment should have made something of himself instead of dwindling into a weak-willed, nerve-racked drug addict. He does not blame his mother wholly for her or his weaknesses, but their world in general. His tortured outburst is enough to affect even the callous observer:

> ... It's not your fault—it's the fault of circumstances and civiliza-
> tion; civilization makes rottenness so much easier. We're utterly rot-
> ten—both of us—... How can we help ourselves? We swirl about
> in a vortex of beastliness....[11]

He is extremely erratic in all his actions and feelings. When he is in one of his quieter moods, he resembles his mother in his persistent craving for admiration. He has never been denied anything in his life, but has wasted every opportunity to prove himself a man of character. He has frittered himself away in the worthless pursuits of his clan, and, while he has had a variety of experiences, he has never learned to appreciate any of the worth-while features of society. When at last he realizes what he has missed, particularly sincere friendship and affection, it is too late, and he is quite justified in reproaching Florence for shirking her responsibility as a mother. Helen, the woman who knows Nicky and Florence better than they do themselves, is the first to guess that Nicky takes drugs. Her admonitions are lost upon him, unaccustomed as he is to kindness and understanding after years of shallow friendships. Tom Veryan expresses a typical attitude of his frivolous set of friends when he comments upon Nicky's place in society: "What's the use of a chap like that? He *doesn't do* anything except play the piano—he can't play any games, he's always trying to be funny—"[12]

The last act, most of which consists of Nicky's denunciations

---

[11] III, 493.
[12] II, 481.

of his mother, is an extremely powerful one. The same brand of bitter earnestness that appears later in *Post Mortem* is to be found here. The atmosphere has been cleared of the "feeling of hectic amusement and noise, and the air black with cigarette smoke and superlatives" which the stage directions for Act Two required. Nicky's cynical reproaches are uttered against a background of silence which enhances their effectiveness. One must perforce pity this twentieth-century Hamlet and his Gertrude for the predicament in which they find themselves, but one is left, nevertheless, as Mr. Coward no doubt intended, with a feeling of disgust for the vapid and futile existence which they have led. Through Nicky and Florence, Mr. Coward passes judgment on the group in which he himself holds membership, and chastizes it for its wastefulness of time, energy, and character. In his accusation of Florence, a speech which seems too long for the usual Coward dialogue, the neurotic Nicky sums up the situation concerning the whole society of idlers:

> . . . . You never love anyone, you only love them loving you—all your so-called passion and temperament is false—your whole existence has degenerated into an endless empty craving for admiration and flattery —and then you say you've done no harm to anybody. Father used to be a clever man, with a strong will and a capacity for enjoying everything—I can remember him like that—and now he's nothing—a complete nonentity because his spirit's crushed. How could it be otherwise? You've let him down consistently for years—and God knows I'm nothing for him to look forward to—but I might have been if it hadn't been for you—[13]

This forceful opprobrium finally subsides into the final scene, in which, after many promises and much commiseration, the curtain is rung down on Mr. Coward's indictment of a social order which accomplishes so little.

The satire in the rest of the play is more in keeping with the usual Coward manner. It is light, flippant, and indulgent, just as we find it in his later and more characteristic plays. Here, too, he is preoccupied with such characters as Pauncefort Quentin, "an elderly maiden gentleman"; Clara Hibbert, a soprano; Tom Veryan, Florence's young athlete; and Bruce Fairlight, the dramatist. These characters represent the customary trappings of a society which deals primarily with the superficial.

---

[13] III, 495.

Pauncefort, or "Pawnie," is included as a means for introducing a few of the bright remarks generally abounding in Coward plays. He talks and acts very much like Oscar Wilde's "Ernest," and makes an art of nonsense. We are to laugh with Pawnie for his facetious comments on the follies of others, but we must laugh *at* him, also, for the feminine attributes with which Mr. Coward occasionally endows certain of his characters. Pawnie is a lover of music and the theatre, and an authority on perfumes (because he uses them), house decoration, and women's clothes. He talks in that staccato rhythm which was typical of Wilde, and is now even more noticeable in Coward. In spite of all his assumed indifference, Pawnie is a sensitive soul. He prefers not to discuss Florence's future, because he is "far too occupied in wondering what's going to happen to me to worry about other people."[14] This is, of course, the cue for Helen's rather unfair rejoinder, "I've always thought your course was quite clear, Pawnie." Pawnie, however, makes light of the apparent offensiveness of the remark. He compensates for his inferiority by being brutally cynical in his conversation.

Clara Hibbert comes in for much of Pawnie's verbal abuse. She is an affected woman who habitually talks in italics. Clara sings at receptions, and is constantly calling attention to that fact. She must have a fan when she performs, because "a fan gives me such a feeling of *security* when I'm singing modern stuff."[15] Her stage fright before the concert is at least partly genuine, but she gets no sympathy from Pawnie, who believes that "she eternally labors under the delusion that she really matters."[16]

Tom Veryan is described by the author as "athletic and good-looking. One feels he is good at games and extremely bad at everything else." He seems out of place in a world where the premium is on brain rather than brawn. A man of few words, because he is not intelligent enough to think of anything to say, he contributes practically nothing to society, not even wit, which in some cases is a legitimate excuse for being. Florence is attracted by Tom's youthfulness, just as he in turn is attracted by her maturity and flattered by her attention. Coward succeeds in creating a handsome man who is void of appeal or interest to the audience.

---

[14] I, 428.
[15] I, 435.
[16] I, 435.

Bruce Fairlight, "an earnest dramatist, the squalor of whose plays is much appreciated by those who live in comparative luxury," is a guest of Florence's because he is a celebrity. The idle rich cultivate celebrities as a matter of course, particularly because there are so many new ones forever cropping up that the novelty does not soon wear off. His seriousness of manner is at odds with the trivial attitude of his hostess and her friends, and his frustrated attempts to enter into grave discussions with these people who mention serious subjects merely for the sake of talking, troubles Mr. Fairlight and amuses the audience.

Throughout the play the concentration is upon the wasted energies and talents in a life given over to the petty concerns of frivolity. The play is not characteristic of the author, for Mr. Coward has long since given up any intentions he may possibly have had of improving his society by calling attention to its emptiness and its weaknesses. *The Vortex* is primarily a play for two characters. The others furnish the necessary background upon which the drama of Nicky and Florence is presented in relief. From this time on, Mr. Coward's depiction of manners and foibles is done with a lighter hand, and the satire, while never lost sight of, is not so scathingly applied.

Hay Fever is perhaps the best known and most characteristic of Noel Coward's comedies. It is a play which has not even the semblance of a plot to distract attention from the steady stream of wit and nonsense pervading it. As in *The Vortex,* the general satire is on the aimlessness of the activities of the *beau monde*. Here again are mirrored the manners of the smart set, a comparatively small and unrepresentative set, to be sure, but always a significant minority. There are people who act and talk like Mr. Coward's characters, but the audience seldom have an opportunity to make their acquaintance in reality. Coward's people are undemocratic and restrict themselves to a world of their own, a world where, as Lamb said, "pleasure is duty, and the manners perfect freedom." In *Hay Fever* the satire is so closely allied with nonsense and farce that it is apt to be overlooked in the ensuing laughter, but this is usually true in comedies of manners, where the comic spirit is ever present.

The duration of the play is from three o'clock on Saturday afternoon to ten o'clock on Sunday morning. In this time the maddest of week-end parties takes place. The action, such as it is, occurs in the home of Judith Bliss, a once famous actress, who is always contemplating a return to the stage. No one in the Bliss household talks sense ; it is against the rules. David, Judith's husband, is a novelist of some note and is usually at work on his new novel, *The Sinful Woman*, although he manages to add his share to the general chaos. The children, Simon and Sorel, are both quite grown up and talented. Simon can generally be found draped over a couch or sprawling on the floor while he works on his sketches. Sorel keeps herself busy by reading poetry or by bothering Simon. The only member of the family who is at all concerned about their nonconformity to the usual conventions, she attempts in vain to reform the others. She is not very successful, and finally decides her efforts are really not worth while. All three are trying very hard to be "landed gentry" in order to humor Judith.

As in the case of Florence Lancaster, the satire is focussed upon the woman who will not accept the fact that she is no longer young but continues foolishly in the ways of her youth. Judith is a woman who, while she loves sincerely her husband and children, is so accustomed to the laudations of the multitude that she considers it her duty to live her own life without tolerating interference from her family. The Blisses, moreover, are far from being an ordinary family.

Simon and Sorel understand and condone their mother's actions, partly because they realize how dull life must be for one who has experienced so many triumphs in the past, and partly because, as Simon says, "people never retire from the stage for long."[17] For this reason they indulge all her whims, or, as Sorel explains to Judith's week-end guest, "one always plays up to Mother in this house ; it's a sort of unwritten law."[18] The life of the Blisses is, accordingly, a highly exciting one, in which, on the slightest provocation, Judith, always aided and abetted by Simon or Sorel, may launch forth into some melodramatic outburst.

Unlike Florence Lancaster, Judith cultivates her affairs with young men not with any immoral motives in mind but for the sake of the adulation involved. When her children criticize her for car-

---

[17] *Hay Fever*, I, 128. (Page references for this play apply to *Bitter Sweet and Other Plays,* Doubleday, Doran and Company, Inc., 1929.)
   [18] II, 176.

rying on with Sandy Tyrell, her latest attachment, her frank response is:

> He's a perfect darling, and madly in love with me—at least, it isn't me really, it's my Celebrated Actress glamour—but it gives me a divinely cosy feeling....[19]

In this way Judith justifies her dabbling in love.

Not for a moment does Judith ever forget that she has been an actress. Not only does she monopolize the center of the stage at all times, but she gets a strange sort of satisfaction from manufacturing effective tableaux and dramatic situations which to strangers are particularly bewildering. Whenever anything displeases Judith, or when her children's criticisms of her threaten to become too numerous, she immediately determines to return to the stage. Thus, when Judith has invited Sandy Tyrell to the house for the week-end, and learns that Sorel has asked Richard Greatham, the diplomatist, to visit them, and that Simon has invited Myra Arundel, the situation becomes rather tense, particularly since each one has planned to use the Japanese Room for his guest. The general confusion which results is added to by David's casual announcement that he has given a similar invitation to Jackie Coryton, a flapper whom he intends to study in connection with *The Sinful Woman,* and that Jackie can, of course, stay in the Japanese Room. Judith very calmly decides she will go back to the stage, and is prepared to defend her decision.

> *Judith.* I'm stagnating, you see. I won't stagnate as long as there's breath left in my body.
> *Sorel.* Do you think it's wise? You retired so very finally last year. What excuse will you give for returning so soon?
> *Judith.* My public, dear—letters from my public!
> *Simon.* Have you had any?
> *Judith.* One or two. That's what decided me, really—I ought to have had hundreds.[20]

The mere idea sends Judith off on a recital of the lines she loved best in *Love's Whirlwind,* while Simon and Sorel assist with the other parts in the melodramatic dialogue.

---

[19] I, 130.
[20] I, 138.

Act Two belongs to Judith alone. Her fatal sense of the dramatic gives her situation after situation which she carries off with a very high hand. The guests are constantly being imposed upon; a family quarrel takes place, and finally all change partners. When Richard, slightly intrigued by her glamour, kisses Judith, the actress in her rises magnificently to the occasion:

> *Judith.* David must be told—everything!
> *Richard (alarmed)*. Everything?
> *Judith (enjoying herself)*. Yes, yes. There come moments in life when it is necessary to be honest—absolutely honest. I've trained myself always to shun the underhand methods other women so often employ—the truth must be faced fair and square—[21]

Richard is amazed at the sudden developments. Judith sweeps out to go to David and stumbles upon Sorel and Sandy in a casual embrace. This time it is Sandy who is startled, while Sorel picks up the cue:

> *Sorel (playing up)*. Mother—Mother, say you understand and forgive!
> *Judith.* Understand! You forget, dear, I am a woman.
> *Sorel.* I know you are, Mother. That's what makes it all so poignant.
> *Judith (magnanimously, to Sandy)*. If you want Sorel, truly, I give her to you—unconditionally.
> *Sandy (dazed)*. Thanks—awfully, Mrs. Bliss.[22]

Judith goes out grandly to have some aspirin, muttering all the while about Youth. Sorel manages to put Sandy at ease by convincing him that nothing that has occurred is to be taken seriously. When Judith next appears, she finds David kissing Myra, and Judith goes into her act again, at the end of which she gives David to Myra, also unconditionally. Myra is frankly scared by the apparent seriousness of the situation which at first had seemed such harmless fun. As David and Judith are saying dramatic farewells to each other, Simon enters from the garden with the news that he is engaged to Jackie Coryton. Judith magnanimously gives Simon to the bewildered Jackie, whose protests are brushed aside. By this time the

---

[21] II, 172.
[22] II, 172.

guests are having a difficult time retaining any traces of sanity which they may have had at the start.   Myra, finally regaining control of herself, becomes their spokesman.   One can almost see Mr. Coward with his tongue in his cheek as he permits Myra to fling out her accusations at Judith and her family.

> *Myra (furiously).* . . . You're the most infuriating set of hypo-crites I've ever seen.   This house is a complete feather-bed of false emotions—you're posing, self-centred egotists, and I'm sick to death of you.
> *Simon.* Myra!
> *Myra.* Don't speak to me—I've been working up for this, only every time I opened my mouth I've been mowed down by theatrical effects.   You haven't got one sincere or genuine feeling among the lot of you—you're artificial to the point of lunacy.   It's a great pity you ever left the stage, Judith—it's your rightful home.   You can rant and roar there as much as ever you like—[23]

In the midst of this pandemonium, Richard, who all this time has been waiting to hear what results Judith's confession of their "love" to David has brought about, enters and very naturally asks : "What's happened?   Is this a game?" not realizing that he is speaking one of the lines from *Love's Whirlwind*.   The Blisses go on from this cue, totally oblivious of their guests, who look on in silent amaze-ment as the curtain goes down.

After this hectic excitement the last act is comparatively quiet. It is Sunday morning ; the Bliss family has got back to normal again, and present a scene of genuine domestic tranquillity.   David is read-ing the final chapter of *The Sinful Woman* to his family while Judith concentrates on newspaper gossip.   An ordinary argument ensues over some unimportant matter, and while all four are talking at once, Myra, Jackie, Richard, and Sandy, not daring to risk an-other meeting with their eccentric hosts, tiptoe out of the house, banging the door after them.   After a few observations on the rudeness of their guests, the Blisses resume their breakfast and their bickering, and the play ends with Judith's final decision that she is really going to return to the stage !

Mr. Coward obviously derived much amusement from cre-ating this satirical study of the middle-aged actress and her family.

---

[23] II, 188.

The satire has not the earnestness prominent in *The Vortex,* but is more in keeping with the indifferent variety generally found in the comedy of manners.

In *Hay Fever,* as in *Easy Virtue,* Mr. Coward consistently satirizes English county society. He mocks their efforts to escape from the inevitable boredom of their existence and is sometimes annoyed by their inane diversions. In *Hay Fever* he devotes the first part of Act Two to the representation of an average after-dinner entertainment. Half-heartedly the group attempt to while away the time by playing "Adverbs," a game which, simple as it is, involves a great deal of explanation and misunderstanding, while each of the guests tries to suggest another game with which he is more familiar. As usual in the Bliss household, general confusion ensues, and a typical family fracas puts an end to "Adverbs."

In *Hay Fever* the characters are playing at being county society; in *Easy Virtue* the characters *are* county society, and, accordingly, Mr. Coward has no sympathy for them. He is merciless in his presentation of a social order which does not quite measure up to the intellectual emancipation of the smart set. Two or three characters who speak Mr. Coward's language are included by way of contrast. He sets side by side the two classes and easily convinces the audience that his own fast-living, free-thinking set is morally superior to a clique which makes fetishes of convention and religion.

Hypocrisy is never tolerated by the members of the smart set, who are essentially straightforward, honest persons. Their moral code, their lack of religious scruples, their casual adulteries may all seem wrong to the majority of observers, but they are willing to face these facts and be truthful about them. Hypocrisy, accordingly, forms the basis for the satire in *Easy Virtue,* because the Whittaker family, with the exception of Colonel Whittaker, are all hypocrites. Mrs. Whittaker and Marion are repressed, narrow-minded women who, by way of compensation for all they have missed in life, devote themselves to meddling in the affairs of other people from what they consider religious motives. Mrs. Whittaker in particular is prejudiced in advance when she learns that her son John has married a woman whom he met at a casino in Cannes. She is certain, therefore, that Larita is a degenerate who is taking advantage of John's wealth and position. Marion, however, is willing to trust in Divine Providence, and is actually looking forward to having a "straight talk to John." Marion is always having straight talks. The Colonel, whose life has been more exciting and whose repressions have been comparatively few, is much more broad-minded than either his wife or daughter, and refuses to judge Larita until he has met her. Mrs. Whittaker and Marion have long since given up trying to reform the Colonel, who, in their eyes, is an old roué whose soul needs considerable saving. Their religious zeal amuses the Colonel since he sees beneath it and knows them for what they really are. His criticism of them is that they "are always trying to help lame dogs over stiles—even if they're not lame and don't want to go."[24] He realizes, too, that subconsciously his wife and daughter look forward to Larita's arrival because it will give them a chance to reform a truly wicked woman. Larita turns out to be a sophisticated, independent person who will not tolerate any dictation in regard to her conduct, and as soon as she becomes aware of the hypocrisy of her husband's family, gives up any intentions of conforming to their standards.

Although Marion dislikes Larita, she insists on being pleasant to her because being pleasant is part of her code. She finds it quite futile, however, to persuade Larita that tennis is better for one than Proust, not realizing that such pastimes as tennis have no place in Larita's world. Her method of deciding what is right and wrong is indicated when she complains to the Colonel about Larita's reading tastes.

> *Colonel (gently).* Don't be sweeping, Marion. Marcel Proust happens to be one of the few really brilliant novelists in the world.
> *Marion.* Pity he chooses such piffling subjects, then.
> *Colonel.* Have you ever read him?
> *Marion.* No—but all French writers are the same—sex—sex. People think too much of all that sort of tosh nowadays, anyhow. After all, there are other things in life.
> *Colonel.* You mean higher things, don't you, Marion?—much higher?
> *Marion.* I certainly do—and I'm not afraid to admit it.
> *Colonel.* You mustn't be truculent just because you've affiliated yourself with the Almighty. (*He goes into the library.*)[25]

---

[24] *Easy Virtue,* I, 19. (Page references for this play apply to *Bitter Sweet and Other Plays,* Doubleday, Doran and Company, Inc., 1929.)
[25] II, 48.

Mrs. Whittaker's crusading spirit does not equal Marion's, but it suffices. Her repressions are apparent in the suspicious way in which she regards everyone else, going so far as to question even the kindly interest the Colonel has taken in Larita. At Mrs. Whittaker's suggestion, Marion has a straight talk with Larita to learn whether or not her mother's suspicions are well founded. After three months of living in the rarefied atmosphere of the Whittaker household, Larita jumps at this opportunity for a scene, and in several impassioned speeches condemns the Whittakers and the hypocritical conventions and prejudices they represent. She considers her past three-months' existence the most demoralizing experience she has ever had, and her indictment of Marion is a harsh one.

> .... You're a pitiful figure, and there are thousands like you—victims of convention and upbringing. All your life you've ground down perfectly natural sex impulses, until your mind has become a morass of inhibitions—your repression has run into the usual channel of religious hysteria. You've placed physical purity too high and mental purity not high enough. And you'll be a miserable woman until the end of your days unless you readjust the balance.[26]

Although Larita still loves John, she realizes that since their return home his love for her has died, partly because of her inability to adapt herself to an unpleasant mode of life, and partly because of John's reawakened interest in his childhood sweetheart. Accordingly, while the Whittaker's long-awaited dance is in full swing, the gorgeously garbed Larita, woman of the world, leaves the house for ever.

The dance itself, supposedly one of the season's events, is a fiasco compared with the party given by Florence Lancaster in *The Vortex*. The Whittaker affair lacks the wit, the superlatives, and the speed which characterized the sophisticated week-end party. Here the people are all dull, although they are the best people of the county, the costumes are ultra-conservative, and the tempo is slow. The guests exchange meaningless remarks as they eat wholesome sandwiches and drink very mild drinks.

John Whittaker likewise comes in for his share of the satire. He has been fortunate enough to break away from his dreary en-

---

[26] II, 89.

vironment, and one hopes that his marriage with Larita will be successful. As soon as he sets foot in the Whittaker house, however, he reverts to type again and takes up the humdrum routine where he had once left it. Toward Larita, John is a cad. He neglects her, leaving her to the antagonism of his family, of which he is hardly aware, while he plays tennis and resumes his friendship with Sarah Hurst, the girl to whom he was once engaged. The sense of security which comes to John from being once again in the bosom of his family leads him to believe that he is secure in his possession of Larita as well. No sympathy is intended for John when his wife walks out of his house; the playwright sees to it that what sympathy there is, is for Larita, a "fallen angel" whose honesty and intelligence make her far superior to the virtuous Whittakers.

The difference between Mr. Coward's smart set and the county society which does not quite measure up to the former's requirements is clearly seen when one considers *The Vortex* and *Easy Virtue* at the same time. Each play satirizes its own clique, but while *The Vortex* to a great extent condones the sins of its characters, *Easy Virtue* holds up to ridicule the weaknesses of its moral paragons.

Private Lives and *Design for Living* continue in the spirit of *Hay Fever* and are more akin to the Congrevean comedy of manners than are any of Coward's other plays. In these plays is reflected Mr. Coward's own set, a society whose members are all as clever as he. Wit and nonsense prod each other in the conversation of these intriguing dilettantes who have no responsibilities, no real business worries, no exacting relatives to deter them from their frivolous pursuits. A world unto themselves, they laugh at moral codes, at religion, at science, and at all the conventions which seem so essential to the rest of civilized humanity. Only a small minority of the audience, those members of the smart set who like to witness the parade of their own foibles, can really affiliate themselves with the characters in Mr. Coward's plays. The best that the others may hope for is that they may be intellectual enough to appreciate and perhaps even envy the cavortings and caprices of the ultra-sophisticated.

Of *Private Lives,* Mr. Coward says, "It is a reasonably well-constructed duologue for two experienced performers, with a couple of extra puppets thrown in to assist the plot and to provide contrast."[27] The leading rôles were taken by Gertrude Lawrence and Noel Coward. *Design for Living* has four important characters, although there are several others who act as foils for them. In commenting upon *Design for Living,* he tells us that he had been contemplating such a play for eleven years, but "it had to wait until Lynn Fontanne, Alfred Lunt, and I had arrived, by different roads, at the exact moment in our careers when we felt that we could all three play together with a more or less equal degree of success."[28] The wisdom of such a delay is apparent in view of the gratifying reception accorded the play and players when they presented it in 1933.

The provocative title of *Design for Living* aroused considerable discussion among the many critics, who, as a matter of course, branded the play as immoral. Mr. Coward, however, has since explained his original intention in presenting to the public this portrayal of life among the artists. "I never intended for a moment that the design for living suggested in the play should apply to anyone outside its three principal characters, Gilda, Otto, and Leo. These glib, over-articulate, and amoral creatures force their lives into fantastic shapes and problems because they cannot help themselves. Impelled chiefly by the impact of their personalities each upon the other, they are like moths in a pool of light, unable to tolerate the lonely outer darkness, and equally unable to share the light without colliding constantly and bruising one another's wings."[29] Mr. Coward's purpose is nothing more than that of mirroring a particular phase of contemporary life which holds itself responsible to no one and, for this reason, gives the audience an impression of extreme moral laxity and degeneracy.

In both plays it is quite evident that although Noel Coward is capable of viewing satirically the irregularities of these impulsive creatures, he is nevertheless very fond of them. Through them, however, he satirizes respected institutions and accepted conventions which to his society are of no value.

In *Private Lives* the situation is a simple one based primarily

---

[27] *Play Parade,* Introduction, p. xiii.

[28] *Ibid.,* p. xv.

[29] *Ibid.,* pp. xvi-xvii.

on coincidence. Amanda Prynne, on the night of her second honeymoon, meets her first husband, Elyot Chase, also on his second honeymoon. The old love returns stronger than ever, and they elope to Amanda's apartment in Paris, jilting their respective mates, Victor and Sibyl. In *Design for Living* there is a recurring juggling of partners, but the situation is a more complicated one, since only one woman is involved in it. The characters concerned are Gilda, an interior decorator; Leo, a playwright; and Otto, a portrait painter. Leo loves Gilda, Otto loves Gilda; Otto loves Leo, Leo loves Otto; and Gilda loves them both. Every attempt to exclude either Leo or Otto from this triangular existence results in failure, and finally, secure in their reciprocal affection, all three come together again. That is the design which troubles the prudish theatre-goers.

The general attitude of these sophisticates in regard to morals is revealed in one of Elyot's reflections on his and Amanda's love. He cautions Amanda:

> *Elyot* (*seriously*). You mustn't be serious, my dear one, it's just what they want.
> *Amanda*. Who's they?
> *Elyot*. All the futile moralists who try to make life unbearable. Laugh at them. Be flippant. Laugh at everything, all their sacred shibboleths. Flippancy brings out the acid in their damned sweetness and light.[30]

His own philosophy of life he also announces, a philosophy which might do well for all the Elyots in his clique:

> ....Let's be superficial and pity the poor Philosophers. Let's blow trumpets and squeakers, and enjoy the party as much as we can, like very small, quite idiotic school-children. Let's savour the delight of the moment....[31]

Otto, too, in *Design for Living,* attempts to convince Gilda that their existence is all right and that they are not loose-living degenerates merely. His argument is:

> ....We are different. Our lives are diametrically opposed to ordinary social conventions; and it's no use grabbing at those conventions

---

[30] *Private Lives,* II, 54. (Page references for this play apply to *Private Lives,* Doubleday, Doran and Company, Inc., 1930.)
[31] II, 54.

to hold us up when we find we're in deep water. We've jilted them and eliminated them, and we've got to find our own solutions for our own peculiar moral problems.... We're not doing any harm to anyone else.... The only people we could possibly mess up are ourselves, and that's our lookout....[32]

Marriage, of course, is laughed out of court in these two plays. Amanda and Elyot attribute their former unhappiness to the fact that they were tied together publicly in marriage, and they do not intend to let marriage again interfere with their love. And when Ernest, the friend of Gilda and Otto and Leo, suggests that Gilda ought to marry one of the two, Gilda explains that the only reasons for her to marry would be to have children, a home, a background for social activities, and to be provided for. But, says Gilda: "I don't like children; I don't wish for a home; I can't bear social activities, and I have a small but adequate income of my own. I love Otto deeply, and I respect him as a person and as an artist. To be tied legally to him would be repellent to me and to him, too."[33] Again, when she is living with Leo, who has become a successful playwright, she laughs at his careless proposal that they marry in order to "ease small social situations," because, paradoxically, marriage would upset her moral principles.

Whenever any of these characters holds forth upon the question of marriage, he generally criticizes the religious principles concerned as well. Amanda's casual reminder that she and Elyot are living in sin encourages Elyot to justify their position according to the Catholic system which does not recognize divorce; and Otto puts all the religious sects on the same plane with the Polynesian islanders, because he feels his conduct is none of their business.

They laugh also at the scientists and mimic the catchwords and phrases used in scientific discussions. The element of satire is indeed conspicuous in the drunken orgy which ensues upon Gilda's temporary desertion of Otto and Leo. The first drink sends Leo off on an oratorical excursion patterned after the best of the soap-box speeches, in which he makes use of the familiar clichés and exhortations. "Science dispels illusions; you ought to be proud to be living

---

[32] *Design for Living,* II, 72. (*Design for Living,* Doubleday, Doran and Company, Inc., 1933.)
[33] I, 10.

in a scientific age." "The time for dreaming is over." "Science proves everything. " But Otto comes back at him with the cynical observation that science is nothing more than "a few tawdry facts torn from the universe and dressed up in terminological abstractions!"[34] Occasionally Mr. Coward's characters even make sport of the achievements in glandular research. Their society is composed primarily of perennially youthful people who require no glandular injections to enable them to retain their zest for living.

Not restrained by any moral codes of their own, they deride the restrictions which the rest of the world place upon each other. Their honesty is constantly being set against the hypocrisy of ordinary citizens who carry on their indiscretions under false pretenses, or, if they lack courage, crush down their emotions and their desires in order to conform to the artificially constructed moral patterns of society. Ernest, the effeminate art collector and connoisseur, gets the brunt of the impact from this trio's perpetual amorous exchanges. Having known all three for years, he feels that he ought to warn them about the consequences of such a lift, but in their eyes Ernest is "nothing but a respectable little old woman in a jet bonnet."[35] Accordingly, they continue to laugh at his admonitions until the time when Gilda, disgusted with Leo and Otto, marries Ernest. The marriage is for Gilda simply an experiment at living a "decent" life and at getting along without Leo and Otto, but it fails the first moment that Leo and Otto reappear on the scene. Ernest, poor thing, argues for morality and decency, and can not be convinced that they are behaving according to their own decencies and ethics. The last scene of the play consists of a series of denunciations by Ernest of this design for living, none of which have any effect upon the reunited lovers.

The character of Ernest is, moreover, a satire on all those persons who, like Pawnie in *The Vortex,* go through life as spectators only. Ernest is an important part in the equipment of this society whose slogan is "Life is for living."

Newspapers in general and the columnists and dramatic critics in particular come in for their share of satire at the hands of Noel Coward. In the informal, lively introduction to *Play Parade,* he

[34] II, 96.
[35] I, 9.

scores off the critics again and again, and mocks the stereotyped phrases which they are wont to use in describing his plays. He delights in his account of the successful reception accorded *Hay Fever*, which the press had described as " 'thin,' 'tenuous,' and 'trivial,' because those are their stock phrases for anything later in date and lighter in texture than *The Way of the World*, and it ran, tenuously and triumphantly, for a year."[36] Accordingly, in his plays, whenever he has the opportunity, Mr. Coward satirizes the critics and their criticisms, and the newspaper columnists as well. In *Hay Fever* he portrays Judith Bliss as taking quite seriously the stupid bits of flattery appearing in a newspaper column of gossip. In *Design for Living* he throws back to the newspaper critics all the customary adjectives and phrases to which he is apparently oblivious. Leo, having just produced a play which to all appearances is successful, cons the morning papers, reeling off to Gilda the usual comments and epithets. Best of all he enjoys the description of the play as "decidedly thin," and Gilda, heartily amused, reminds him that the *Daily Mirror* "means to be kind. That's why one only looks at the pictures."[37]

Mr. Coward likewise takes to task the typical newspaper interviews with which celebrities are constantly confronted, when he has a reporter ask Leo the usual trite questions. Leo impatiently flings out his answers to the barrage of queries about the talkies, the modern girl, and marriage, and permits the reporter to take a picture of him. In *Point Valaine* Mr. Coward turns the tables on Hilda James, the reporter who has followed Mortimer Quinn, the novelist, to the island for an interview with him. Instead of permitting her to question him about his likes and dislikes, the novelist upsets all the conventions and finally has the silly girl confiding all her hopes and ambitions, much to his own amusement and to her surprise.

People who achieve success in any profession are not generally well liked by the members of the smart set, who are content to lead a careless life which does not involve contacts with the outside world. Leo and Otto lose Gilda when they attain success. Theirs is a small world which admires talent, but recoils from public recognition of it. Thus, when Gilda appears to be lost to them, they

[36] *Play Parade,* Introduction, p. xi.
[37] *Design for Living,* II, 38.

plan vengeance on the whole social system by taking advantage of
all the superficial accoutrements of success, the photographs, the
interviews, the secretaries, fur coats, and dressing-gowns. Leo
vows not to allow "one shabby perquisite to slip through our fingers !"[38]

Noel Coward's impatience with dullness is expressed through
his creation of such characters as Victor Prynne, Mr. and Mrs.
Carver, and the numerous guests who sit and talk on the porch of
Linda Valaine's hotel. Victor is a wooden, pompous individual
who finds himself suddenly married to the exciting Amanda. He
loves her, but not in the impulsive manner of Elyot Chase. He is
extremely polite and solicitous, just the opposite of Elyot, and is no
match for Amanda in temperament and ingenuity. Lacking any
imagination, he can not play up to her moods and can not recognize
when Amanda is joking. From the start, one feels intuitively that
Amanda is making fun of him, nor is one sorry for him when she
leaves him for Elyot.

One expects the Carvers to be stupid, prosaic people, since they
are friends of Ernest. They are at Ernest's house when Leo and
Otto arrive to claim Gilda, who at the moment is showing the house
to another friend. Leo and Otto are in excellent spirits, and the
entire scene is immediately effervescent with their good humor and
their mad-waggery. The Carvers, never having met such mischie-
vous effrontery, are at a loss to know how to cope with the intru-
ders. Etiquette tells them that they must keep up a conversation
at any cost, but their attempts in this direction meet with disastrous
results when Leo and Otto take over the conversation. Helen Carver, in an effort to be friendly, inquires if they are old friends, and
is startled when Otto replies nonchalantly that they lived with Gilda
for years. Lacking a sense of humor, the Carvers listen seriously
to the nonsense. Leo's discovery that the Carvers have been married two years is the cue for a serio-comic discussion of youth and
love.

> *Otto.* There's something strangely and deeply moving about
> young love, Mr. and Mrs. Carver.
> *Leo.* Youth at the helm.
> *Otto.* Guiding the little fragile barque of happiness down the

---

[38] II, 95.

river of life. Unthinking, unknowing, unaware of the perils that lie
in wait for you, the sudden tempests, the sharp jagged rocks beneath
the surface. Are you never afraid?

Henry. I don't see anything to be afraid of.

Leo (fondly). Foolish headstrong boy.[39]

When Gilda comes downstairs with her friend, Grace Torrence,
the situation is tense. Gilda, as soon as she conquers her surprise at
seeing Leo and Otto, tries vainly to restrain their exuberance, although she knows she has no power over them. Finally, by means
of their audacious epigrams and topsy-turvy generalizations, they
rout the bewildered Carvers and Miss Torrence from the house.

In *Point Valaine* Mr. Coward continues his satire on the duller
members of society by recording in detail the insignificant dialogue
and the trivial concerns of the guests at Linda Valaine's hotel.
They spend their time talking about liver pills, mosquitoes, and
jellyfish, much to the delight of Mortimer Quinn, who is casting
about for material for a forthcoming novel. The inconsequential
chatter of five or six girls about hats and young men is in decided
contrast to the intelligence of Linda Valaine and Mortimer Quinn,
and serves as a somewhat transparent screen for the serious drama
of love and passion going on in the house. *Point Valaine* is not to
be considered a typical Coward play, however. It is included in
this discussion because of the few bits of satire which relate themselves to the satire in *Private Lives* and *Design for Living*. The
main figures in *Point Valaine* are earthy, sensual creatures who
illustrate the most unpleasant aspects of life in the tropics, and
who could not, because of their corruptness of character, and because of the influence of the extreme climate, engage in the banter
and caprices of the smart set.

---

[39] III, 112.

SUMMARY

The chief concern throughout this study has been to point out how important a rôle satire has played in the dramatic works of Congreve, Sheridan, Wilde, and Coward, and in what respects these writers resemble or differ from each other in their comedies of manners. Congreve, breaking away from Elizabethan traditions to adopt the continental play-writing techniques imported by Charles II and his court from France, looms large as an innovator with regard to this dramatic type. Sheridan, Wilde, and Coward in turn are successful representatives of the Congrevean school for their respective periods, and their satiric comedies differ according to their times in both matter and manner. Congreve's five-act plays are much heavier in texture than any of the later plays considered. In them he satirizes pleasure-loving Restoration society for the most part through his characterizations. One play alone, as has been pointed out, might contain satire of numerous characters, fashions, and foibles. Sheridan, on the other hand, is more generous, frequently using an entire play to satirize one particular weakness of his age, as in *The School for Scandal* and *The Rivals,* where he shows up, respectively, slander and sentimentality. Oscar Wilde's satire finds expression in the verbal achievements of his characters. Noel Coward resembles Sheridan in that he devotes an entire play, such as *Easy Virtue* or *Design for Living,* to the ridicule of Victorian prudishness or the insignificance of present-day moral conventions. Also, he is close to Wilde in that he is invariably clever and flippant.

The plays of all four men mirror admirably the superficialities of sophisticated upper-class society, and at the same time reflect definite changes in moral tone. The licentiousness of Congreve's gallants, stifled by the diatribes of the conscience-stricken Jeremy Collier, gave way to a stiff, cautious morality, then dwindled into middle-class sentimentality. The ensuing drama was the result of an unexciting life in which intellectual stimulation was negligible. In Sheridan's plays the spirit of Congreve's comedies made a transitory appearance, and vanished in the wake of coming romanticism. After nearly a century of domestic tragedies, melodramatic spectacles, and other bourgeois bills of fare unconducive to satire and wit, it returned again in the plays of Oscar Wilde. Victorianism was losing its influence in the last decades of the nineteenth century, and the reaction made itself felt in Wilde's portrayals of a society which had restored wit and artificiality to their proper places. There were many attempts to imitate the brilliance of Wilde, but not until the present day do we find again the real comedy of manners. The intervening war years brought a frankness and worldliness which resemble most nearly the outspokenness of Congreve's day. Noel Coward's characters, in their disregard of moral codes, in their sophistication, and in their effervescent spirits, are indications that the temper of contemporary society is in closer relationship with that of the Restoration period than with that of any other since Congreve.

Modern English comedy begins with Congreve and continues unretarded in Sheridan and Wilde. Coward, representing a reversion to the freedom of the Restoration, rounds out a complete cycle in the history of the comedy of manners.

VITA

Rose Snider was born October 16, 1912, in Portland, Maine. She entered the University of Maine from Portland High School in 1929 and was graduated four years later as a member of Phi Beta Kappa and Phi Kappa Phi. Awarded a Trustee Fellowship for graduate work in English, she undertook as a thesis subject for her Master's degree, granted in 1936, an investigation of satire in the comedies of Congreve, Sheridan, Wilde, and Coward, which is the basis of this study. In 1935-36 she was assistant in English, and in 1936-37, instructor, in the University of Maine.

BIBLIOGRAPHY

EDITIONS OF THE PLAYS

Congreve, William (1670-1729)

Ewald, A. C., ed. *The Complete Plays of William Congreve*. The Mermaid Series. New York, Charles Scribner's Sons. [n. d.]

Coward, Noel (1899-)

Coward, Noel. *Bitter Sweet and Other Plays*. New York, Doubleday, Doran and Company, 1929. [*Easy Virtue, Hay Fever, Bitter Sweet*]

Cavalcade. New York, Doubleday, Doran and Company, 1933.

Conversation-Piece. New York, Doubleday, Doran and Company, 1934.

Design for Living. New York, Doubleday, Doran and Company, 1933.

Fallen Angels. London, E. Benn, 1925.

The Marquise. London, E. Benn, 1927.

Play Parade. New York, Doubleday, Doran and Company, 1933. [*Design for Living, Cavalcade, Private Lives, Bitter Sweet, Post-Mortem, The Vortex, Hay Fever*]

Plays. First Series. New York, Doubleday, Doran and Company, 1928. [*The Queen Was in the Parlour, Home Chat, Sirocco*]

Point Valaine. New York, Doubleday, Doran and Company, 1935.

Post-Mortem. New York, Doubleday, Doran and Company, 1927.

Private Lives. New York, Doubleday, Doran and Company, 1930.

The Rat Trap. Contemporary British Dramatists. Vol. 13. Boston, Le Roy Phillips, 1924.

Tonight at 8:30. New York, Doubleday, Doran and Company, 1936.

Sheridan, Richard B. (1751-1816)

Hamilton, Clayton, ed. *Plays by Richard Brinsley Sheridan*. New York, The Book League of America, Macmillan Company, 1929. [*The Rivals, St. Patrick's Day, The Duenna, The School for Scandal, The Critic*]

Wilde, Oscar (1854-1900)

Comedies by Oscar Wilde. New York, The Book League of America, 1932. [*The Importance of Being Earnest, Lady Windermere's Fan, An Ideal Husband, A Woman of No Importance*]

WORKS CONSULTED

BOOKS

Aldrich, Mrs. Thomas Bailey. *Crowding Memories*. New York, Houghton, Mifflin Company, 1920.

Beer, Thomas. *The Mauve Decade*. New York, Garden City Publishing Company, 1926.

Bernbaum, Ernest. *The Drama of Sensibility, 1696-1780.* Boston, Ginn and Company, 1915.

Brown, John Mason. *Letters from Greenroom Ghosts.* New York, Viking Press, 1934.
  The Modern Theatre in Revolt. New York, W. W. Norton and Company, 1929.

Burdett, Osbert. *The Beardsley Period.* London, John Lane, The Bodley Head, 1924.

Cannan, Gilbert. "Satire." *The Art and Craft of Letters.* London, Martin Secker. [n. d.]

Chandler, Frank W., and Cordell, Richard A. *Twentieth Century Plays—British.* New York, Thomas Nelson and Sons, 1934.

Clark, Barrett H. *A Study of the Modern Drama.* New York, D. Appleton and Company, 1928.

Collier, Jeremy. "A Short View of the Immorality and Profaneness of the English Stage." Spingarn, J. E., ed. *Critical Essays of the Seventeenth Century.* 3 vols. Vol. III. Oxford University Press, 1909.

Coward, Noel. *Present Indicative.* New York, Doubleday, Doran and Company, 1937.

Cunliffe, John W. *Modern English Playwrights.* New York, Harper and Brothers, 1927.

Dickinson, Thomas H. *Contemporary Drama of England.* Boston, Little Brown and Company, 1931.

Dobrée, Bonamy. *Restoration Comedy, 1660-1720.* Oxford, The Clarendon Press, 1924.

Doran, George H. *Chronicles of Barabbas.* New York, Harcourt, Brace and Company, 1935.

Filon, Augustin. *The English Stage.* New York, Dodd, Mead and Company, 1897.

Garnett, Richard. "Satire." *Encyclopaedia Britannica.* 14th ed. New York, 1929.

Harris, Frank. *Oscar Wilde: His Life and Confessions.* New York, Garden City Publishing Company, 1930.

Lamb, Charles. "On the Artificial Comedy of the Last Century." *Essays of Elia.* New York, Lamb Publishing Company, 1899.

Lewis, Lloyd, and Smith, Henry Justin. *Oscar Wilde Discovers America.* New York, Harcourt, Brace and Company, 1936.

Meredith, George. *Essay on Comedy and the Uses of the Comic Spirit.* New York, Charles Scribner's Sons, 1907.

Nathan, George Jean. *Art of the Night.* New York, Alfred A. Knopf, 1928.
  Passing Judgments. New York, Alfred A. Knopf, 1935.

Nettleton, George H. *English Drama of the Restoration and the Eighteenth Century, 1642-1780.* New York, Macmillan Company, 1914.

Nicoll, Allardyce. *An Introduction to Dramatic Theory.* New York, Brentano's, 1924.
  British Drama. New York, Thomas Y. Crowell Company, 1925.
  History of Early Eighteenth Century Drama, 1700-1750. Cambridge (Eng.) University Press, 1925.

History of the Late Eighteenth Century Drama, 1750-1800. Cambridge (Eng.) University Press, 1927.

Restoration Drama, 1660-1700. 2nd ed. Cambridge (Eng.) University Press, 1923.

Palmer, John L. *Comedy of Manners.* London, M. Secker, 1914.

Renier, G. J. *Oscar Wilde.* New York, D. Appleton-Century Company, 1933.

Robinson, F. N. *The Complete Works of Geoffrey Chaucer.* New York, Houghton Mifflin Company, 1933.

Sawyer, Newell W. *Comedy of Manners; from Sheridan to Maugham.* Philadelphia, University of Pennsylvania Press, 1931.

Swinnerton, Frank. *The Georgian Scene.* New York, Farrar and Rinehart Company, 1934.

Taylor, D. Crane. *William Congreve.* Oxford University Press, 1931.

ARTICLES IN MAGAZINES AND NEWSPAPERS

Atkinson, Brooks. "Present Indications." New York *Times,* Section 11, p. 1, April 11, 1937.

Carmer, Carl. "Noel Coward: 'Good Theatre' in Modern Dress." *Theatre Arts Monthly,* 17:198-205, March, 1933.

Corbin, John. "Noel Coward." *Saturday Review of Literature,* 9:445-446, February 25, 1933.

Furnas, J. C. "The Art of Noel Coward." *The Fortnightly Review,* 140: 709-716, December, 1933.

Haraszti, Zoltán. "William Congreve." *More Books,* 9:81-95, March, 1934.

Nathan, George Jean. "Art of the Night." *Saturday Review of Literature,* 15:16, April 17, 1937.

News-Week, p. 22, July 13, 1935. [Item about performance of *The Country Wife* in Connecticut]

Nichols, Lewis. "Noel Coward Presents the Design for His Own Living." *New York Times Book Review,* p. 3, April 4, 1937.

Watts, Richard, Jr. "The Success Story of a Man of the Theater." *New York Herald Tribune Books,* p. 4, April 4, 1937.

Woodward, Frances. "Popularity and Noel Coward." *Saturday Review of Literature,* 15:5, December 19, 1936.

INDEX

Satire in Coward
  The smart set, 102-113, 116-117;
  county society, 113; hypocrisy,
  113-116; social conventions, 116-
  119; marriage, 119; religion,
  119; science, 119-120; morals,
  120; newspapers and critics, 120-
  121; success, 121-122; dullness,
  122-123
Satire in Sheridan
  Sentimentality, definition, 43-44;
  romantic sentimentality, 44-47;
  moral sentimentality, 44, 47-51,
  52-53; hypocritical sentimentality, 44, 51-55; pretensions to education, 57-61; female gossip,
  62-64; male gossip, 64-67; senile
  love and jealousy, 67-70; country
  people and manners, 70-71; duelling, 71-73
Satire in Wilde
  Typical representatives of the
  smart set, 78-82; pretensions to
  wit, 82-83; clergy, 83-84; servants, 84-85; gossip and hypocrisy, 85-86; spinsters, 86-87;
  false values of society, 87-89;
  marriage, 89-90; arranged marriages, 90-92; education, 92-93;
  America and Americans, 93-94;
  puritans, 95-96; the "other
  women," 96-97
Saygrace, Mr., 34
Scandal, 7, 29, 39
School for Scandal, The (Sheridan),
  22, 41, 42, 44, 62, 124
Scoundrel, The (Hecht and Mac-
  Arthur), 100
Sensibility, Comedy of, *see* Comedy
  of Sensibility
Sentiment, 43 (definition), 51
Sentimental Journey, A (Sterne),
  44, 45
Sentimentality, 43-44 (definition),
  51, 53, 55, *see also* Satire in
  Sheridan
Setter, 33-34
Shakespeare, 18
Sharper, 21, 27, 28
Sheridan, Richard B.; Foreword,
  iii; Introduction, vii, ix, x; bio-
  graphical sketch, 41-43; discus-
  sion of satire in Sheridan, 43-73
  (*see* Satire); Sheridan and Con-
  greve, 22, 41, 42, 43, 44, 53, 56-
  57, 58, 59, 62, 65, 68, 69, 70;
  Sheridan and Wilde, 74, 77, 82,

85, 90; Sheridan and Coward,
  98, 99-100, 102; Summary, 124-
  125
Shirley, James, 11
*Short View of the Immorality and
  Profaneness of the English
  Stage,* A (Collier), 33, 34
Sinful Woman, The (Bliss), 109,
  110, 112
Silvia, 11, 20-21, 28
Sampson, Sir, 7, 29
Snake, 51-52, 63, 64, 65
Sneer, 56
Sneerwell, Lady, 49, 51-52, 62-67
Snider, Rose, ii, iv, 126
Spaniards in Peru, The (Kotzebue),
  43
"Speranza," 74
Spintext, Parson, 23
Steele, Richard, 71
Sterne, Laurence, 44
Suckling, 37
Sullivan, Sir Arthur S., 93
Surface, Charles, 49, 52, 53, 54, 63,
  66, 67, 68
  Joseph, 44, 51-55, 63, 64, 65, 66,
  67, 68
  Sir Oliver, 55, 66, 68

Tattle, 36, 38, 39
Teazle, Lady, 57, 63-64, 65, 67, 68-70
  Sir Peter, 22, 54, 63-64, 65, 66, 67,
  68-70
Terence, 18
Thomas, 44
Thraso, 18
Tom Thumb (Fielding), 55
Tonight at 8:30 (Coward), vii, 99
Tophas, Sir, 18
Torrence, Grace, 123
Touchwood, Lady, 11-13
  Lord, 12
Tribulation Spintext, 33
"Tuppy," 80, 83
Tyrell, Sandy, 110, 111, 112

United States, Oscar Wilde on the,
  93

Vainlove, 4, 5, 11, 20, 21
Valaine, Linda, 122, 123
Valentine, 3, 6-7, 18, 29, 33, 35, 38,
  39-40
Veitch, Violet, 98
Veryan, Tom, 103, 105, 106, 107
Victorian, ix, 124
Voltaire, 1